BY WILLIAM WISTAR COMFORT

WILLIAM PENN AND OUR LIBERTIES

THE PENN MUTUAL
LIFE INSURANCE COMPANY
INDEPENDENCE SQUARE
PHILADELPHIA   PENNSYLVANIA

"It is taken for granted that every American school-boy ought to know something about William Penn, because he colonized one of the States. It is not enough to know that he organized and financed the settlement of Pennsylvania. It is assumed that every American ought to learn something about the man in order to understand our national history. The fact that Penn was a Quaker, the status of Quakers in England during his life, Penn's personal relations with the King—such matters are regarded as properly a part of American history, since they make it more easily understandable."

—GERALD W. JOHNSON.[1]

"Pennsylvania may well be proud of such a founder and lawgiver as William Penn, and an obligation be felt by her enlightened citizens to cherish by commemorations of his exalted philanthropy and his beneficent institutions, their expanding influence in the cause of civil and religious liberty."

—JAMES MADISON IN 1826.[2]

I

FOR Americans the Liberty Bell is a symbol, a sacred relic. It is the only one they possess, except the flag, of such universal appeal. A symbol may be defined as a visible sign of something invisible. Liberty is an abstract quality which cannot be graphically portrayed. Yet everyone wants it. So the Liberty Bell is treasured by the nation as a symbol of the liberty that has already been attained and of the future liberty yet to be realized.

A few words will suffice to connect this national treasure in Philadelphia with the Founder of Pennsylvania, William Penn. Recent research has shown that though the date on the Bell is 1753, it was ordered in 1751 by the superintendents of the State House, one of whom was Isaac Norris Jr.[3] This Isaac Norris was born in the Slate Roof House at the corner of Second and Sansom Streets in 1701, the son of Isaac Norris the intimate friend and associate of William Penn. The younger Norris entertained a special reverence for the great friend of his father. Moreover he was born in the year of Penn's Charter of Privileges in 1701, when Penn about to leave Philadelphia for the last time had granted a constitution which endured until the Revolution. The year 1751 when the Liberty Bell was ordered by the younger Norris and his associates was then the fiftieth anniversary of Norris' birth and also of the final colonial constitution of Pennsylvania.

Now it will be remembered that the inscription on the Bell reads: "Proclaim Liberty throughout all the land unto all the Inhabitants thereof. *Lev.* XXV, vs X." If we examine this Biblical text, we find that in its entirety it reads: "And ye shall hallow the fiftieth year, and proclaim liberty throughout all the land unto all the

[3]*All reference notes are grouped on pages 141, 142, 143*

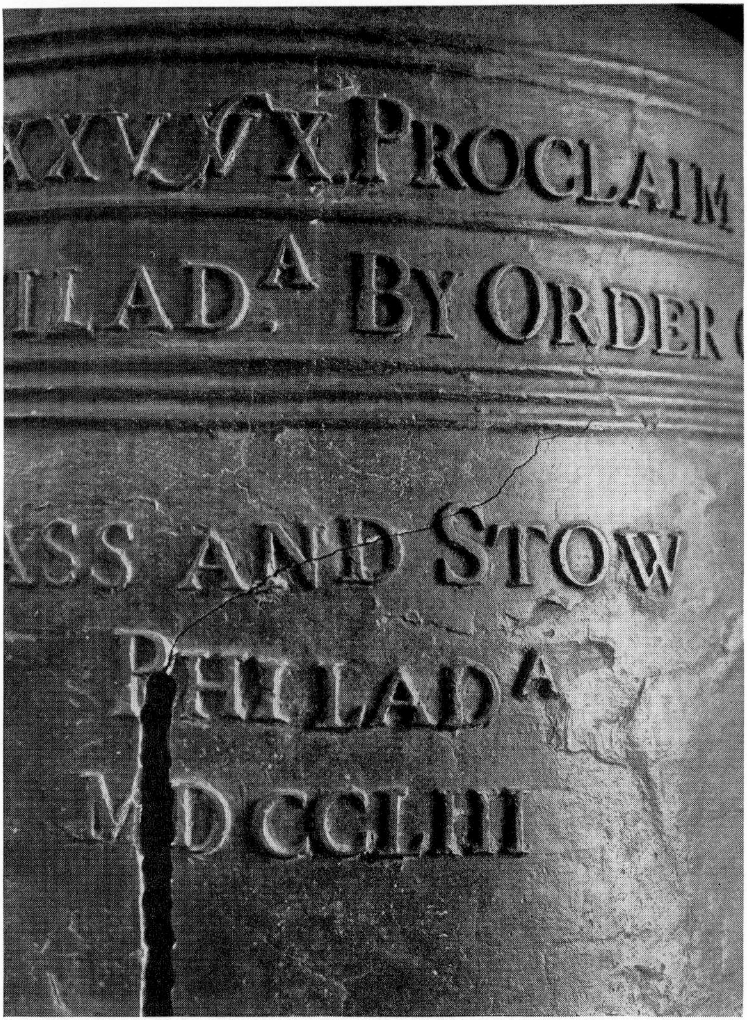
XXV.V X.PROCLAIM
ILAD.A BY ORDER
ASS AND STOW
PHILADA
MDCCLIII

inhabitants thereof: it shall be a jubilee unto
you; and ye shall return every man unto his
possession, and ye shall return every man unto
his family."

We see thus that the fiftieth year was a year
of jubilee to be kept sacred, when every man
should recover his possessions and his family
fireside. According to the Lord's instructions
to the Children of Israel, this jubilee was thus
to be inaugurated fifty years after entering the
Promised Land. It was to be hallowed as a year
of rejoicing for blessings received, when all
oppression of one man by another should cease
and every man should return unto his possessions.
We do not know who selected the text for the
inscription. But the sense of it is plainly one
of rejoicing that liberty of the spirit had been
attained and that men were free to seek their
soul's desire.

In 1753, when the Liberty Bell was finally
received from the founders in England, twice
recast, and placed in the tower of the State
House, there was the French and Indian war
still to be fought, and some years were to elapse
before there was any question of severing the

ties of the colonies with the mother-country. The connection of the Liberty Bell with political independence in 1776 is therefore entirely fortuitous: the big bell in the State House was simply the one nearest at hand when the hour of jubilation came.

What the Liberty Bell originally symbolized, then, was the freedom of spirit and liberty of conscience which Penn had bequeathed through a series of charters and privileges to his citizens in Pennsylvania. These privileges cherished in constitutional form in 1701 became the frame upon which the Articles of Confederation and the later Constitution of the United States were built. These Articles and this Constitution were framed and subscribed in Philadelphia, in the very building over which the Liberty Bell swung. But it is only by chance that the Bell is associated with the declaration of independence from England. This fact, indeed, clinched its hold upon the imagination of posterity. But few people now need to be reminded of the Declaration of Independence. That page of history is closed.

The Liberty Bell, however, was not hailed

by that name, according to Dr. Stoudt, until 1839. In that year The Friends of Freedom published in Boston a sonnet bearing that title and distributed it at the annual fair of the Massachusetts Anti-Slavery Society. From that time for several decades the Bell became a symbol of the anti-slavery movement. That page too is closed.

What we need to recall now and to retain is the freedom of conscience and the civil rights which are our heritage, and which the Liberty Bell was first cast to commemorate. This national heritage comes to us Americans pre-eminently through William Penn, the Founder and Lawgiver of Pennsylvania, between 1681 and 1701.

Philadelphia has three patrons under whose name and protection its business is carried on: William Penn, Benjamin Franklin and Stephen Girard. These names have been chosen because of their local significance to Philadelphians, and because they are synonymous with honesty, integrity and solidity. A glance at a telephone directory will offer convincing evidence that any establishment from a bank, insurance company, club, college or hotel to that of a butcher and baker, if not a candle-stick maker, does business under the aegis of one of these remarkable men. Penn suggests comparative antiquity and Quaker integrity, Franklin suggests broad and practical humanitarianism, and Girard suggests great wealth wisely bestowed. In other American cities there is no parallel for the manner in which these three men monopolize the nomenclature of Philadelphia's business.

Yet, none of them was born a Philadelphian. In 1644 Penn could not have been born in a city which did not yet exist. Franklin born in Boston could not feel at ease in the Puritan capital and chose the Quaker city for its congenial atmosphere of freedom and its eighteenth-century enterprise; if he stayed longer in Boston, he says, "I might . . . soon bring myself into scrapes; and further, that my indiscrete disputations about religion began to make me pointed at with horror by good people as an infidel or atheist." Girard, born in Bordeaux, found here a centre from which he could direct the creation of his great fortune later devoted to the welfare of the city.

The character and genius of the three men

were very different, and our knowledge of them varies greatly. Franklin is the most popular and the best known of the three. He himself told us much of what he wanted posterity to know, he possessed traits and qualities which endear him to the American, and his patriotic role in colonial America is impressed upon every schoolboy. He was part of American history in the making, and he is claimed by the entire country. Girard is far more local in importance, but several recent biographies have revealed the character of this strange foreigner, the generous disposition of whose vast estate has brought the blessing of education to generations of Philadelphia boys.

Popular knowledge of Penn suffers from the fact that he lived so long ago in a social and political arena which is quite beyond our ken. He was a man of the seventeenth century, as Franklin was of the eighteenth, and Girard essentially of the nineteenth. That fact makes a good deal of difference. We can know exactly how Franklin and Girard looked, for example; but despite several representations of Penn, some of which are fanciful and spurious, we cannot see him as he looked when he first sailed up the

Delaware in the *Welcome* in 1682 at the age of thirty-eight. On the other hand, thanks to the State's reconstruction of Pennsbury Manor on its original lines, we can see now how Penn the Quaker country-gentleman and governor lived near Bristol on the Delaware. Moreover, the little house now removed to Fairmount Park is also a reminder of the domestic life in the early years of Penn's town. Beside correspondence and legal documents, Penn left 2000 folio pages of religious, moral and political treatises, to be found now only in large libraries. Franklin wrote much less but very significantly. Girard wrote for posterity not at all.

The result of this brief comparison of the knowledge attaching today to our three patrons is that Penn's personality and contribution to history is the least known of the three. Despite the efforts made in connection with the recent Tercentenary of the Founder's birth, the man walking up Broad or Market Street knows only that that is a statue of "Billy Penn" up on the City Hall, that he was a Quaker and founded Pennsylvania. It seems that the city fathers felt satisfied when they had once hoisted the 37 foot bronze statue five hundred feet *above* the city pavements. As a result, there are few people down *in* the streets who know what they owe of civil liberty and religious freedom to this Quaker Founder. Penn would have liked to be nearer to his people than he is. He longed to be understood by them. For this purpose, a book in the hand may be more informing than a statue in the air.

© Photo Illustrators.

II

IT is important to know just what William Penn's part was in the establishment of religious freedom and of democratic civil rights in America. It is of no service to make extravagant claims for him or to assert that if it had not been for him, we should never have developed in America the ideals that we cherish. There were so many other groups of people beside the Quakers who came to America in search of the same freedoms that Penn sought that sooner or later both religious and civil rights would have been claimed by colonists in America.

But Penn, rather than any other individual

founder or colonist, proved to be the chosen vessel through which the stream of demand for respect of individual rights was to flow so richly into our American reservoir of precious ideals. He was the agent for carrying across the seas certain ideals which were impossible of realization in seventeenth-century Europe. He felt, as he said, that these ideals had a better chance of realization in America than in Europe. He would try the experiment. It would be his "Holy Experiment".

The yearning for religious liberty is older than the struggle for civil liberty. To confine ourselves to the Christian era alone, it is evident that the early Christians, though persecuted for their religion, had no thought of political revolt against their imperial masters. Indeed, their very religion itself, based on their Lord's instructions, distinguished nicely between respect for constituted authority and the rights of conscience: Caesar had his rightful claims and God had his.

So it continued through the Middle Ages. The many individual and group protests of Christians in favor of individual rights in matters of faith and practice were made against the tyrannical authority of the mediaeval church, and not against the powers of the state. Only where the church had come to control the state and dictate its policy toward alleged recalcitrants, was the authority of the state involved in the protests of its Christian citizens. The rights of "the powers that be" were recognized by Christians within limits as being inviolable until comparatively recent times: "the powers that be are ordained of God," St. Paul had said to the Romans.

By the sixteenth century the authority of church and state was so completely fused in many European countries that a crime against one was regarded as a crime against the other. By the Roman Catholics, and very soon also by the Protestants and Reformers, the state found itself forced to punish alleged sins of commission and omission against the church which exercised control over the national religion. The church became very literally the power behind the throne, and from that protected position called the signals. Thus, civil liberties and religious freedom were alike threatened and were placed in the same jeopardy.

The history of modern religious toleration is the story of man's insistence that church and state should be divorced. There was little desire for genuine democracy in Europe before the eighteenth century. But there was a steady demand for liberty of conscience already in the wake of the Reform movement. And this statement makes no mention of the earlier Albigenses, the Waldensians, the Poor Men of Lyons and other mediaeval groups who had claimed the right to worship God as they thought right without interference from the church of Rome. By this church they were regarded as heretical and were persecuted as such.

It should be recalled for our present purpose that the great religious movement which we call the Protestant or Reform movement was at first a protest against existing abuses in the Roman Catholic church, a demand for a reform rather than an absolute divorce. For a long time this movement did not concede full freedom of conscience or liberty of worship to the nationals of regions where it prevailed. Some courageous and freedom-loving souls thus felt that the Reformation had not gone far enough, had proved to be political rather than spiritual, and had stopped short of attaining those privileges of religious freedom which some few prized more than life itself.

There was, indeed, a line of "spiritual reformers" in western Europe during the sixteenth and seventeenth centuries, men who lived such a life and preached such a gospel as they believed was given them by God to live and to preach, regardless of what an established church might think or decree against them. Neither Calvin nor Luther was comfortable in the presence of these men who reminded them of the shortcomings of the great movement identified with their names. These spiritual reformers all headed little groups of congenial spirits who felt that they had been let down by the titled Reformers.

These little groups formed the original crusaders for religious liberty in modern times. They were followers of Boehme, Denck, Frank, Castellio, Schwenkfeld, Menno Simons and others still less known today.[4] Though leaders and adherents were persecuted and exiled by the Protestant heads of church and state, they carried on in western Germany and in the Low

Countries. When all looked dark for freedom
of conscience and liberty of worship, even under
a Protestant dispensation, they kept a light burn-
ing which has now become as bright as the day-
light itself; when the opposing line of prejudice
and bigotry was most deeply entrenched, they
carried the ball again and again to score the gains
by which we have profited.

The names of these men are almost unknown
today except to historians. Only the Schwenk-
felders and Mennonites have survived in num-
bers, and they came to live in our midst. For it
was natural that in the eighteenth century these
sturdy German descendants of an uncompromising
tradition should have been attracted by the
pronouncement of a Quaker in 1701 that in his
province "no person or persons . . . shall be in
any case molested or prejudiced, in his or their
person or estate, because of his or their conscientious persuasion or practice, nor be compelled to frequent or maintain any religious
worship, place or ministry, contrary to his or
their mind, or to do or suffer any other act or
thing contrary to their religious persuasion."
Such a declaration must have brought cheer to

religious groups which had been badgered and
chevied about like criminals by their lords
spiritual and temporal. They came to Penn's
woods and have stayed.

But what of Penn? How did he come to hold
these advanced ideas of religious freedom? We
must connect Penn and his English Quakers with
the liberal tradition which we have found suffering but existing on the Continent.

In England, as on the Continent, there had
been long before the Reformation such significant
movements as that of Wycliffe's Lollards. By
1547 when Henry VIII threw off the papal rule
for reasons of his own convenience as a much-
marrying man, there was plenty of popular
support for his action. Henry's religion was
called by a contemporary "a medley religion",
and Penn later called the King himself "an
hermaphrodite in religion". The King's decisions
and deeds were hardly consistent or defensible,
but they were colorful and have given the dis-
traught young student of English history something tangible and memorable to lay hold upon.
Jacques Barzun mentions the despairing professor
of history who exclaimed from the heart "Thank

God for Henry VIII!" This king, however, whose life was so unedifying and whose religion was such a "medley" that he executed Protestants and Catholics with impartiality, nevertheless started something. He established a national church independent of the Pope, in whose face he thus snapped his fingers. And by making this epochal break with Rome, he opened the way for other smaller religious groups to assert independence of authority in matters of conscience and manner of worship.

As we have seen, there were little groups of religious people in western Europe who ran neither with the Catholic nor the Protestant pack. These groups belonged to an invisible, unorganized communion, in most cases distinctly mystical. They placed their confidence in a direct personal revelation of truth and of their duty; their ministry was lay and unpaid; they cherished the Bible as the text-book they were bound to know; their life was simplicity itself; many of them would neither fight with carnal weapons nor use oaths; they were inured to persecution; they went their own way and were consequently suspected and hated by both church authorities and Protestant princes. As Penn later remarked, "Persecution entered with creed-making,"[5] and the simple independent faith of these plain people made them an easy mark. However, a few leaders among them such as were named above preached and wrote books through which their religious ideas gained currency.

These ideas made their way to England through personal contacts and literary channels, and there found a fertile soil. Once the thraldom of a universal communion had been thrown off, the way was open for all independent elements in the population to assert themselves. And this was true of those who rebelled against the coercion of the newly-established Anglican church as well as those who renounced Catholicism. In plain words, there were many people in England who would have no more of their own established church than they would of that of Rome.

There was thus great confusion by the middle of the seventeenth century. Political events of course reflected the religious confusion. Penn lived through it all under Charles I, the Puritan Commonwealth and the emergence of the Independents, the restoration of Charles II, James II, William and Mary, Queen Anne and George I. It was a time when modern religious ideals of freedom and democracy were beginning to assert themselves with new vigor. Appeal was being made to Magna Charta in support of the people's rights, and Penn himself constantly invoked the "good old admirable laws of England" in favor of religious toleration.

Under William and Mary the worst abuses of intolerance were corrected, but during the middle decades of the century England presented a religious bedlam. Catholics, Anglicans, Presbyterians, Independents, Baptists, Anabaptists, Brownists, Familists, Unitarians, Muggletonians, Levellers, Ranters and finally just "Seekers", were some of the religious groups which divided the population about 1650. Not the good life but a water-tight creed was the concern of many of these groups. When caught in the jam of a political upset, it was easier to trim sails by changing one's creed than to improve one's morals. For many servants of religion the important thing was to make a valiant show of a certain creed until one's living was at stake, and then to change the creed. Between Henry VIII and Charles II one may imagine how many tuft-hunters had to change their colors.

The late A. Neave Brayshaw's excellent book on *The Quakers* (N. Y., 1938) quotes an anecdote which underlies the well-known song about the Vicar of Bray: "This vicar," says Brayshaw's authority, "taxed by one with being a turncoat and an unconstant changeling: 'Not so,' said he, 'for I have always kept my principle, which is this, to live and die the vicar of Bray.'"

In all this confusing welter there were men giving serious thought to the problems of religion and of state in England. Some were divines, university-trained men acquainted with Platonism and disciples of the Continental humanists who reclaimed for man the sense of direct communion with a Spirit that dwelt within him and to whom was his first allegiance: i. e. the kingdom of God is in the heart of man. The names and contribution of these Englishmen who carried into our immediate tradition this profound sense of privilege and responsibility are readily accessible. They form the learned link with the Continental spiritual reformers to whom reference has already been made.

In the history of ideas, such a link of learned minds has always proved to be indispensable. It is true that so long as dynamic ideas remain cloistered up in universities they will not disturb society. But when they escape and establish contact with the needs of society outside, then something will happen, there will be action. Society feels the expanding power of a new idea when it once "takes". Charles I was not the only man to lose his head at the demand of one idea in 1648; nor was Sir Harry Vane the only one to lose his head a few years later when another idea prevailed. The times were pregnant with progressive ideas struggling with reactionary theories of control, and heads were dropping on both sides. Little by little the Stuarts and all that they represented were revealed to the nation as a reactionary force which must be driven from the land before there was a chance for liberal democracy to take shape.

It was during this struggle, when Parliament was striving to regain its representative rights from two monarchs who fought for their lives, pleasures and prerogatives from 1660 to 1688, that Penn was at the height of his powers and was working on plans for New Jersey and Pennsylvania. He was not aloof on the side-lines of the field; he was in the midst of the struggle, writing, speaking and going to prison for his testimony. He knew personally the royal protagonists of one theory and had access to their presence; but he also knew and sympathized with the leaders of the more excellent way that eventually triumphed,—the way of such men as Algernon Sidney, John Locke and others who were affected by the gentle and liberal views of the Cambridge "Latitude Men". Most important of all for us, he knew George Fox.

Professor A. W. Whitehead recently remarked (*Adventures of Ideas*, 1933, p. 63): "The apostles of modern tolerance so far as it exists are Erasmus, the Quakers and John Locke. They should be commemorated in every laboratory, in every church, and in every court of law." Erasmus and Locke are great names in the struggle for toleration, but their reputation is abundantly able to take care of itself. Since we must confine ourselves here to tracing our own special line of descent, we must turn now to Penn and indicate

at some length the significance of his acquaintance
with Fox and with the Society of Friends or
Quakers which Penn joined at the age of twenty-
three.

Born in 1624 of a humble but respected family
in Leicestershire, George Fox was innocent of
any higher education. He placed no confidence
in the university training which at that time was
held to be a necessary qualification "to be
ministers of Christ." He eschewed the subtleties
of theology. He was unquestionably an extraordinary person both physically and spiritually.
Physically he endured persecution and exposure
which would have killed many a man. Spiritually
he is regarded by modern historians of religious
movements as having expressed one of the
authentic varieties of religious experience.

To gain this experience he, like Penn, had to
wait for twenty-three years. These years were
spent in search and struggle. Being a godly
youth, he was revolted by the smug hypocrisy,
simony and insincerity of the preachers whom he
went to hear. In discussions with some of them,
he received strange replies to his troubled questions: one advised him to "take tobacco and sing

psalms"; another proposed to "give me some physic, and I was to be let blood"; his relatives "would have had me marry". He did none of these things at the time, but kept on praying for relief in agony of soul. We find in his *Journal* the brief account of the annunciation to him personally:

> "And when all my hopes in them and in all men were gone, so that I had nothing outwardly to help me, nor could I tell what to do, then, oh! then I heard a voice which said, 'There is one, even Christ Jesus, that can speak to thy condition': and when I heard it, my heart did leap for joy. Then the Lord did let me see why there was none upon the earth that could speak to my condition, namely, that I might give Him all the glory; for all are concluded under sin, and shut up in unbelief, as I had been, that Jesus Christ might have the pre-eminence, who enlightens, and gives grace and faith and power. Thus when God doth work, who shall hinder it? And this I knew experimentally."[6]

The important feature of this experience is that it was personal, direct and certain. Henceforth, Fox had the great asset of certainty that he was right, that he had heard for himself, without human intermediary, the divine assurance that God was with him and in him. The will of God as revealed to him would henceforth show him what was right and what was wrong in a great many matters which other Christians of the day felt to be outside of the divine purview. The immediate connection between faith and works henceforth proclaimed by Fox was very aggravating to the conventional professors of religion, many of whom had established that comfortable divorce between profession of faith and a godly life which prevails to the present time. Fox discovered that religion was not confined to creeds and outward sacraments, but that it entered daily life at every moment. It was man's chief business to keep "on top of the world" and all its temptations and to place himself at God's disposal. Hence Quakerism is often called "a way of life," because it set out to follow the dictates of a God-illumined conscience.

It is evident that the adoption of this principle by Fox separated him and his later adherents from all the existing institutional religion of the churches, Catholic, Anglican, Presbyterian, Independent or Baptist. In fact, Quakerism is not primarily a church, but a "movement", a Society of Friends, as the modern name implies. It was formed at first and is still formed today by seekers who feel that other churches are too vicarious, that they place too much between God and the worshipper. Fox and the early Publishers of Truth whom he sent out from the north to preach all over the British Isles, in America, on the Continent and in the near east, were carried on with the rushing conviction that they had something which would save men from that formality and insincerity which were rife in the organized churches of their day. All idolatry, hypocrisy, mere lip-service and time-serving they condemned, not in order to make Quakers, but to save individual souls. They bade men to deny ungodliness and worldly lusts and to live soberly, righteously and godly in this present world. What they preached was mysticism, but a practical mysticism to be recognized in a changed way of life.

It is always impressive to see in the history of religious movements how a stricter discipline, a heavier burden, is gladly welcomed and shouldered by some. It was so with the Seekers who listened in the squares, inn-yards and orchards to the out-door itinerant preaching of the early Quakers. There was no collection taken up, no rousing song-service, no appeal to come to the mourners' bench, no bid for membership in a religious group. There was silence and then just an *ad hominem* appeal to "come off" from the world and its vain glories and heed the call of the divine voice within.

It was such an appeal in a meeting of Quakers at Cork in 1667 which reached William Penn, when Thomas Loe proclaimed that "there is a faith which overcomes the world, and there is a faith which is overcome by the world." For, like so many others, Penn was a seeker. He was unsatisfied by the Anglican church into which he had been baptized at birth in London, and he had seen more than enough of the world and its gay society in London, in Ireland and in France. For him there was no further doubt or hesitation,

as there had been none twenty years earlier for
Fox. He knew what he was doing, what the price
would be in the loss of worldly preferment, but
he valued the precious spiritual peace all the
more because of the high price he paid for it.
Without bearing a cross, there would be no crown.

Before looking more closely at what has been
called "the making of William Penn", we must
now say a little more about the tenets, principles
and testimonies held by these inconspicuous
members of the middle and lower classes whose
lot the eldest child of a worldly Admiral had
decided to share.

Quakerism at the start was absolutely evan-
gelical. Its business was to call sinners to re-
pentance, to save their souls and the soul of the
nation. Like the Old Testament prophets, Fox
believed and preached that God was wroth with
the accumulated evils of a wicked and adulterous
generation and that He would wreak vengeance
upon those with whom He was displeased. This
belief was, of course, perfectly orthodox in
accord with the religion of the times. The
Puritans had entertained the same convictions,
but Fox could not see that they had corrected

the abuses which he saw all about him. Instead
of quarrelling over theological dogmas, it was
time, Fox felt, to bring religion into personal
lives and thus raise the standard of national
morality.

What was new and significant was his teaching that there was "that of God" in every man,
something divine implanted in everyone which
he often called "the Light", "the Witness" or
"the Seed". This "Seed" or divine element was
indeed corrupted and mortified by the fall of
man, but it could be revived and made effective
in any man by that abundant and effective grace
of Christ which Paul said had "appeared to all
men." Though Fox himself did not feel called
to engage in theological disputations, it is evident
that he here ran afoul of the Calvinistic teaching
of the time that such grace was limited to a
chosen few, and that all others were doomed to
feel the effects of original sin.

The Quakers, for their part, have always
believed in universal grace and are what the
theologians call Arminians. The consequences
of what thus appears at first to be a mere theological question over which school-men have dis-

puted through the centuries from Paul and
Augustine to Calvin and the Catholic Jansenists,
are profound. We shall meet some of these consequences later, for they affected inevitably the
dealings of Penn with some of his greatest problems.

The belief in a divine seed or principle in
every man is also a deciding factor in favor of
toleration. Such a belief equalizes all men as
sons of God, as brothers one of another. "The
other fellow" is as worthy of consideration as
oneself. He may be wrong, but he must be
"labored with" until convinced at heart, and not
slain or forced by the weight of sheer power to
an unwilling and superficial confession of defeat.
Thus, Fox exhorted his Friends to live so as to
answer the Witness of God in every man, that
is, apply the Golden Rule universally and without reservation. This principle, if applied, requires time, great patience and forbearance. It
has distinguished the attitude of the Quakers
toward war and capital punishment, and has often
caused them to be misunderstood by their fellow-
citizens. They feel that anything short of a
change of heart in one's adversary is worth

nothing and cannot be trusted.

Many other people hold today that this change of heart can be effected in a nation by the timely use of atomic bombs, or by mass executions or by economic strangulation or by a reformed national education. The Quakers, provokingly allergic to individual or mass hatreds, preached love and good will to all, striving to live "in the virtue of that life and power that took away the occasion of all wars." The danger of preconceived judgments is constantly brought home to us in these modern days. Friends have held, with Penn, that "if it be an evil to judge rashly or untruly of any single man, how much a greater sin it is to condemn an whole people."[7] So their methods of dealing with criminals or with enemy peoples are preventive, curative and conciliatory in the belief that such methods are more befitting professed Christians and in the end more effective. Penn gives the reason for this attitude when he says: "We say a measure of divine light is in every transgressor, even at the instant of his committing the vilest sin, yet it consents not to it, but stands a witness for the Lord God against the unrighteous soul."[8]

It will be seen now what wide ramifications
in life will be affected by this belief in the sacredness of human life and in the inviolability of the
individual conscience. Penn held that "Conscience is God's throne in man, and the power
of it his prerogative",[9] and "Liberty of conscience is every man's natural right."[10] Because
of these concepts, Penn asserted that "No man
is so accountable to his fellow-creatures as to be
imposed upon, restrained, or persecuted for any
matter of conscience whatsoever."[11] The fact is,
of course, that under the Restoration men *were*
being imposed upon, restrained and persecuted
for just this reason. For in 1680 there was presented to King Charles II, lords and commons
in parliament assembled "The Case of the People
called Quakers", in which it was stated that in
the preceding twenty years alone, that is since
the Restoration, there had died in prison, been
imprisoned, excommunicated or sentenced to
banishment, (not for crimes against the state
but for purely conscientious refusal to conform
to the penal acts in force to compel religious
conformity), a total of 10,778 persons.[12] We
have the records which show how accurately

the score was kept by the suffering Quakers.
Penn himself was in prison once in Ireland and
at least three times in London for writing, speaking and acting as a Quaker. From his first sojourn
in the Tower he wrote "My prison shall be my
grave before I will budge a jot, for I owe my
conscience to no mortal man."[13] We may look
for the guarantee of religious toleration to be
writ large at the very heart of Penn's later plans
for his province in the New World. He had seen
enough of intolerance to know that "Whatever
the persecuted be, the persecutor, to be sure, is
always in the wrong."[14]

In those days men lived in a world of dual
loyalties. A man enlisted on one side or the other.
There was recognized to be an unreconcilable
enmity between the interests of this world and of
the world to come, between the temporal and
the eternal. It is not easy for us today, who have
done so much to reconcile good and evil in the
same life, to appreciate the vast difference this
distinction of loyalties would make in the life
of a conscientious man. It accounts for the
extreme position taken in the seventeenth century
by men who strove to live in the power of an

endless life. To them this world and its lure was to be eschewed, and this life was to be lived as if it was to be eternal. Penn held that "he that lives to live ever, never fears dying."[15] He also wrote "If God's presence makes the heaven . . . then since God vouchsafes to temple and tabernacle in men, it follows that his heaven is there also."[16] The seriousness of life comes home to anyone who believes that Christians are called to be perfect. Unremitting attention to the Light Within every man would lead him to the Truth. In the quaint phraseology of the day, the Seed of the woman was destined to bruise the seed of the serpent. The pertinent question then was whether one should ally himself with the seed of eventual death and destruction or with the seed of life and power. As Fox wrote as early as 1652: "If ye hearken to the Light in you, it will not suffer you to conform to the evil ways, customs, fashions, delights and vanities of the world; and so lead you to purity, to holiness, to uprightness, even up to the Lord."[17]

The early Friends felt that they were very favored persons, but the favor brought with it serious responsibility. As Fox wrote in a general epistle, like St. Paul in this respect, "The Lord doth require more of you than he doth of other people; because He hath committed more to you . . . The world also expects more from Friends than from other people; because you profess more."[18] Penn was conscious of the same responsibility: "Friends, this know, we are the people above all others that must stand in the gap, and pray for the putting away of the wrath, so as this land be not made an utter desolation; and God expects it at our hands."[19] Enough has been quoted to show that the early Quakers like the early Christians were perfectionists. They felt obligated to leave undone what they ought not to do, and to do what ought not to be left undone. This conviction, often expressed with more force than tact, was one more cause for their early persecution. It is never pleasant to feel reproved by the life of someone who is doing better than we are.

There is one further feature of the Quaker philosophy which meant much to Penn's later theory of government. It was the belief in "a continuing revelation" of God's will to those who sought to know it. This is the opposite of "a closed revelation", according to which the revelation of God's nature and purpose in the life of Jesus Christ as recounted in the scriptures was final. This latter interpretation, so current still among Christians, confines our attention to the scriptural portrayal of the historical Jesus, and focusses our desire upon an objective attempt to realize in our times the standards proclaimed by Him. For some this is a difficult exercise, and the world has been quick to decide that times have changed, and that the standards of Jesus have frozen and are no longer practicable. The Quakers, like some other Christians, held that at all times God had revealed, and was ready now to reveal, through the Inward Light what his will was concerning us. As the ancient Jews conceived of God as talking and walking with the heroes of the Old Testament, so the Quakers held that He would talk and walk with us today. Their identification of Jesus with the eternal Word of *John I* made Jesus to them coeternal with the Father. The Christian dispensation terminated a religion of sacrifices and burnt offerings, but it neither began nor ended the solicitude of God for man as preeminently evidenced in the sacrificial life of his Son. Far from minimizing the role of the historical Christ, as some of their contemporaries maintained, the Quakers thus extended both backward and forward in time the significance of Him who was once manifested in the flesh but who always templed in the heart of those who would give Him place.

A few quotations from Penn's writings will make clear his practical application of this conception: "Salvation was salvation, and a child of God a child of God, in all ages;"[20] "Christ was before the law, under the law, with the prophets, but never so revealed as in that holy manhood;"[21] "By good reason may we conclude that Christ is an immediate perpetual speaker to his Church;"[22] "Christ, the Word-God, has lighted all mankind, not only after his coming in the flesh, but before;"[23] "Who walked in the light in any age so far walked in the counsel of God. And that all mankind had an ability from God so to do, is our belief;"[24] "The great foundation of our Protestant religion is the divine authority of the Scriptures from without us, and the testimony and illumination of the

Holy Spirit within us;"[25] "God raised us up, and we are now gone forth into the world to declare that He is spiritually manifested, as then fully in that body, so now measurably in the consciences of all people, a divine light, reproving every unfruitful work of darkness;"[26] "In all ages hath the Almighty more or less pleaded his own cause in the consciences of all people by this divine principle of light, however variously denominated."[27]

Enough has been said to make clear the point so vitally important to Penn, that human life is, and always has been, by its very nature wrapped up in and subject to the divine will. Not only the individual's welfare but that of the nation is dependent upon righteousness and obedience to the divine will. One of Penn's most familiar sayings in his first Frame of Government thus becomes intelligible: "Government seems to me a part of religion itself, a thing sacred in its institution and end." Enough has also been said to prove that any consideration of the liberties and privileges which we Americans owe to Penn is incomplete unless we show the immediate and the remote religious tradition to which he belonged. He will attempt to apply his religion to government.

Soon after his "convincement" of Quakerism in 1667, Penn became a mighty preacher of the Truth as he understood it, in the meetings of the Friends or Children of the Light. Reference has already been made to those assemblies of Seekers who at the beginning of the movement gathered in the open air to stand in silence waiting to hear Fox or some of his associates speak to them the words of life. A few years later meeting-houses began to be built in the cities and country, and we may think of Penn for the most part as sitting indoors with his brethren and taking an active part in the spiritual exercises of the company. These meeting-houses were then as now severely plain, for as Penn said, "God's presence is not with the house, but with them that are in it, who are the Gospel church, and not the house."[28] Seventeen years earlier George Fox tells in his *Journal* of having been pushed about in a church and told to get out by a zealous parishioner:

"Alas, poor man!", said I, "dost thou call the steeple-house the church? The church is the

people, whom God hath purchased with his
blood, and not the house."[29]

Fox was an unlearned man, and Penn was
highly educated. But despite the frequent difference in their language, one can recognize
Penn in Fox on every point where their interests
coincided. Penn was thus not a detached individual, but one of a compact and like-minded
Society.

The nature of these Quaker meetings for
worship was determined by the Quaker faith
in the leadings of the Inward Light, the Christ
Immanuel in whose honor they were met. The
ministry was free and not paid, it might be
exercised by man, woman or child, and it must
be prompted not by human "notions", but by
divine inspiration only. Here was liberty indeed.
From the start Quaker worship then has been
distinguished from that of other Christians. In
one of his admonitory epistles in 1657 Fox
expressed it concisely: "If any have any thing
upon them to speak, in the Life of God stand
up, and speak it, if it be but two or three words,
and sit down again; and keep in the Life, that
ye may answer that of God in every man upon

the earth. To you this is the word of the Lord God." The solemnity of silence broken by inspired words may be very deep. Many have testified to the profound impression produced by such an occasion.

Penn's future father-in-law, Isaac Penington, found peace, as Fox had done, in silent waiting: "This is he, this is he; there is not another, there never was another. He was always near me, though I knew him not . . . Oh! that I might now be joined to him, and he alone might live in me." The aristocratic Robert Barclay, known as the early Apologist of Quakerism, says it was not by strength of arguments or any disquisition of doctrine that he was convinced; but "when I came into the silent assemblies of God's people, I felt a secret power among them, which touched my heart, and as I gave way unto it, I found the evil weakening in me, and the good raised up, and so I became thus knit and united with them." In 1795 Stephen Grellet, the great Franco-American Quaker, when describing the first Friends' meeting he attended on Long Island, used substantially the words of Penn a century before, when he says: "Seeking for the divine presence, I was favored to find *in* me, what I had so long, and with so many tears, sought for *without* me." It was in such meetings which he attended with the greatest regularity twice or more a week that Penn found his inspiration and strength. His later friend, Isaac Norris after being at meeting with him in London, noticed that despite all Penn's troubles and anxiety at the time about his private affairs, "his foundation remains."

Having now shown that Penn did not stand alone, but that he belonged to a people who, more than most, brought religion into daily life, we may now turn our attention to other factors in his life which account for his personality and the part he took in developing our American ideals.

III

THOUGH this is in no sense a biography of William Penn, consideration of the important factors in the development of the Founder of Pennsylvania will give an opportunity to touch upon certain features of his active life. In addition to the significance of his being a Quaker, which must be constantly emphasized, there are five other contributing causes which make him the man he was and enabled him to do what he did. It is true to say that for lack of any one of these contributing causes he would not have become what Lord Acton called "the greatest historic figure of the age."[30]

The first of these was his birth,—not his
physical birth, of course, but the social position
into which he was born at a critical period in
English history. He was born into the upper
middle class. The Penns had been country-
gentlemen for some generations, but his father
was a distinguished Admiral in the British navy
and was later knighted. The later favor shown
to this Admiral by the two Stuarts, Charles II
and James Duke of York whom he served,
enabled his son to associate with whom he
pleased. Throughout his life he could choose
his friends either above or below him in the
existing social scale. The list of his friends
and correspondents includes such names as Sir
Bulstrode Whitlock, William Popple, John Locke,
Algernon and Henry Sidney, the Lords Halifax,
North, Culpepper, Baltimore, Rochester, Rane-
lagh, the Earl of Sunderland, the Duke of Ormond, his sons the Earl of Ossory and the Earl
of Arran, King Charles II and King James II.
Some of these important social connections he
owed to the distinction and favor won by his
father, and some of them he owed to his own
affable personality and his later prominence as

a colonial Proprietor. These aristocratic connections were an important asset. There was no other contemporary Quaker, except Robert Barclay, who could have mingled with men of such lofty social and political flight. Barclay was for several years titular Governor of East New Jersey, but he never visited America and died at the early age of forty-one.

Penn's specifically intimate relations with the Duke of York, later James II, form a very interesting chapter in the Quaker's experience. The Admiral at the time of his death had committed William to the good offices of the Duke. This charge the Duke later kept with conspicuous fidelity. But there was also a personal attraction between these two men so different in their ideas; for while James as King headed the Catholic party at court, Penn was spokesman and advocate for the Quakers and others under persecution for violation of the Penal Laws. Yet both men were interested in terminating the persecution of their co-religionists, and this community of interest drew them together. Penn was repeatedly called a Jesuit himself and was later placed in jeopardy because of this very friendship for James. He never denied this friendship, but is said to have admitted that "King James had always been his friend, and his father's friend; and that in gratitude he himself was the King's, and did ever, as much as in him lay, influence him to his true interest."[31] Penn certainly sought nothing for himself at court, and for this James was grateful. We should remember that this King, whose reputation in history is none of the best, was perhaps the deciding influence in determining his brother Charles II in 1681 to give Penn the province he asked for in America. A little later he even added to the original grant the ducal possessions now represented by the State of Delaware, but in the early days of Penn's experiment called "the lower counties."

To the friends at court and in Parliament mentioned above should be added the great number of his co-religionists to whom Penn was known through his extensive preaching missions and his colonial projects. He was a loyal, generous and exuberant friend who did not fail to let others know when he felt kindly towards them. Among those in the little town of Philadelphia whose friendship he most valued in early days of the city were Edward Shippen the mayor, Isaac Norris, Thomas Lloyd the first president of the Provincial Council, Phineas Pemberton, Caleb Pusey, Griffith Owen, Thomas Story, Samuel Carpenter and James Logan. His correspondence with these men both individually and collectively should be read for an estimate of his wide interests and incessant activities.

This mention of his activities introduces the thought of Penn's sustained good health and strong constitution. Few men are called upon to exercise such continuous activity in private and public affairs as he from 1681 until his illness incapacitated him in 1712. Notable are his four journeys to the Continent, the first one being for prolonged study as a youth in France, and his two visits to America. The sea voyage in little sailing vessels of those days might consume from four to twelve weeks, and the peril from storms, pirates and the enemy was equalled by the discomfort and the danger of disease in such confined quarters. It will be remembered that one-third of the hundred passengers in the *Welcome* died on the western passage, and that

Penn's "singular care was manifested in contributing to the necessities of many who were sick of the small-pox." It is not necessary to rely upon the tradition of his outjumping Indians at their games in order to credit Penn with unusual strength and vigor. Through all the vicissitudes of extended travel, through the strain of frequent preaching missions in England on horseback and the exacting details of his distant colonization plans and the financing of them, we hear of no serious illness until the repeated strokes which impaired his mentality between 1712 and 1718. He was the first child of youthful parents and had himself apparently fourteen children born to his two wives. To live in possession of all his faculties for sixty-eight years at the pace he set entitles him to some distinction as a strong man.

A man's education is of the greatest importance in determining his attitude toward such problems of public import as were to be faced by William Penn. His preparation for the role he was later called upon to play was remarkably adequate. We may examine in some detail what this preparation was. As a lad he attended an excellent

WM. PENN

grammar school near London, was later taught by private tutors, and in 1660 at the age of sixteen entered Christ Church at Oxford as a "gentleman commoner". Here he appears to have shown spirit, but not of a kind which was valued by the authorities. He doubtless learned much, but rebelled against the Anglican control which had just been reestablished at the University by the Restoration. He joined with other students of Puritanical persuasion and resisted the requirements of chapel attendance. For this he was "sent down", or as he says "banished the College". Years later he referred to "my persecution at Oxford" and always preserved an unhappy and perhaps prejudiced memory of his undergraduate days. Not lacking in the use of the vituperative language so common in his day, Penn in 1670 addressed this masterpiece of scurrility to the Vice-chancellor of Oxford University: "Poor Mushroom, wilt thou war against the Lord, and lift up thyself in battel (*sic*) against the Almighty?"[32]

Oxford not having been a success, his enraged father sent Penn with a small party to the Continent, where the youth elected to spend about

eighteen months at Saumur, the site of the leading French Protestant seminary of the day. It
is significant that a short stay in the gay capital
of Louis XIV sufficed for this serious-minded
youth, and that he chose rather a provincial
place of prolonged residence where he could
associate intimately with one to whom he owed
so much. This was the great Protestant theo-
logian Moïse Amyrault. It is certain that at
Saumur he became familiar with the Church
Fathers and gained that knowledge of Church
history which served him well in his later polemics
with churchmen. At this time he gained a spoken
knowledge of French. Of course, Latin and
Greek he possessed from his school and university days. By the age of twenty Penn had certainly gained a book education equal to what he
would have obtained by a longer residence at
Oxford, and far superior to that of the average
American student of his years.

Because of a threatening war with the Dutch
the Admiral recalled his son to London in 1664
in time to witness the Great Plague, the Great
Fire and the Dutch war. Pepys, a friend and
neighbor of the Penn family, refers in the churlish

fashion he so often adopts in his Diary to William's return: "I perceive something of learning
he hath got, but a great deal, if not too much,
of the vanity of the French garb and affected
manner of speech and gait. I fear all real profit
he hath made of his travel will signify little."[33]
His wife, who was half French herself, thought
him "a most modish person, grown a fine gentleman."[34] He must have presented a manly figure
with his rapier and clothes of fashionable cut,
and his new command of the popular Continental
tongue. The Admiral, at last, was pleased with
the success of his son's grand tour.

A brief study of law at Lincoln's Inn intro-
duced Penn to a field in which he later showed
proficiency on many an occasion. The Admiral
was now at the peak of his fame. As Great
Captain Commander he commanded the sea
forces under the Duke of York when the Dutch
were defeated in 1665. Having accompanied his
father to sea, William was sent back with dispatches from the fleet to the King's presence,
and from that time could command, if he chose,
the attention of the two royal brothers. This
was quite in line with the ambition of his father

that his eldest child might have an entree at court and attract the favor of the King. But he made no use of this favor for eight years.

A further step in his training as a man of the world was a visit to the Shangarry estates which the Admiral had received from Charles II in exchange for the estate at Macroom, also in County Cork, with which Cromwell had previously endowed him. Penn thus had the practical experience of administering for some months his father's Irish property. Finally, as a complete historical anomaly, he served in the militia under the patronage of the Duke of Ormond, helped to put down a local uprising at Carrickfergus, was commended to his father, and had his portrait painted in armor! This is the period when, as he later wrote, "the glory of the world overtook me."[35]

Such in briefest words was the story of the "making" of William Penn. He was well made for his future career. Though he had done nothing remarkable at the age of twenty-three, he was "all set" for the brilliant future at court or in administrative councils which the Admiral had planned for him. The disappointment over

the Oxford fiasco was forgotten in the apparent
success which had crowned other steps in his
"making". There could have been nothing observ-
able up to this time which threatened the steady
progress toward preferment which the Admiral
had plotted for his son.

Then the unexpected happened, and all the
future appeared to crash. For under the gay
exterior of this fashionable young gentleman
there was an unsatisfied demand. The society
he had seen in the two most civilized countries
of Europe left him cold. However much his
mind had been enlarged, his heart had not been
touched. It was now ready at the age of twenty-
three to be set on fire. He had certainly heard
of the Quakers before 1667, as any intelligent
person must have heard of them, and it is certain
that he had heard before the itinerant Quaker
preacher who reached him now in Cork.

The decision to associate himself with a
humble people whose very religious meetings
were at this time unlawful was immediate and
final. He was promptly arrested at a meeting
and jailed with others for his presence there,
but was later released when his identity was

disclosed in a letter to his father's intimate friend, the Duke of Orrery, then Lord President of Munster. Even this untoward experience was of educational value, for he hereby learned what religious intolerance was at first hand. For the next twenty years he fought intolerance and persecution for conscience' sake at every opportunity with tongue and pen.

It is well to understand what was to be the inevitable result of Penn's association with the Quakers. His manner of life, language and society would immediately be altered. Not his theology was at stake, but his way of life. Everything for which his life had been planned was now beyond his reach. He had eliminated himself from all possibility of preferment in court and government circles. He of course knew this as well as his father did. In 1681 he wrote: "I have been these thirteen years the servant of truth and Friends, and for my testimony sake lost much, not only the greatness and preferments of this world, but 16,000 pounds of my estate, that had I not been what I am I had long ago obtained."[36] Again in 1689 in a general epistle to Friends he reminds them: "It is now about twenty-two

years since I embraced the testimony of the
blessed truth, and the fellowship of it among
you, which is Christ, the light of the world,
in us, the hope of the glory that is to come. I
cannot repine, notwithstanding the many sort of
troubles and afflictions I have met withal on that
account, whether they came from my near
relations, or the governments of the world, or
my neighbours, or my enemies, or my false
friends."[37]

On hearing of his son's doings in Cork, the
Admiral lost no time in sending for him. He had
a fine rod in pickle for William's arrival in
London. When his son addressed him with the
"plain language" used by the Quakers, his
father told him "he might thee and thou whom he
pleased except the King, the Duke of York and
himself." The Admiral's ire was more justified
on this occasion than in 1662 when he had whipped,
beaten and turned his son out of doors because
of his banishment from Oxford. But such corporal
chastisement would be hardly fitting if applied
to a young man of twenty-three. The Admiral,
used to Spartan discipline, was nonplussed by
his son's action, as he realized that all his fond

dreams of a brilliant future for William were ended.

The good will which characterized his new-found religion prevented any hard feeling on the part of William for his father, and it is pleasant to learn of their later mutual understanding and reconciliation shortly before the Admiral's early death in 1670 at the age of forty-nine. In record-ing the interview some years later in *No Cross, No Crown*, the son thus quotes his father: "Son William, if you and your Friends keep to your plain way of preaching, and keep to your plain way of living, you will make an end of the priests to the end of the world." Doubtless William felt completely vindicated by such a frank ap-proval of the Quaker position.

These remarks anent the Admiral bring us to the fortune he left his eldest child in addition to the respect and honor due to his professional reputation. The landed estates left by the Admiral yielded an annual income in rents of fifteen hundred pounds. The purchasing power of money being then three or four times as much as now, William was left in possession of a very con-siderable fortune. He was able in the next ten

ADMIRAL PENN.

One of Cromwell's Admirals who took

Jamaica from the Spaniards

from the Original Picture

London Published by R.N.

years to marry, have a country-place, raise a
family, travel widely on preaching missions,
spend some time in prison, and make two visits
to Holland and Germany. At no time in his
life did Penn have to work for a living. He was
one of the richest young men in the Society of
Friends. He could associate with any Quakers
and with many of the "world's people", but all
avenues of advancement in government were
closed to him.

And now we come to the last and greatest
factor in determining the historical importance
of William Penn. Without it he might have been
remembered as a great force in securing religious
toleration in the English-speaking world. Without it he would certainly have been one of the
three or four greatest names in the history of
Quakerism. But without it Pennsylvania would
never have received its name or its character,
nor would Penn have become one of humanity's
signal benefactors. For it is only fair to remember
that if Penn made Pennsylvania, Pennsylvania
also made Penn a truly historical figure. When
he secured Pennsylvania, he secured the greatest
opportunity any single man ever had to found a

state in which his own ideas should be realized. That these ideas were determined by the other factors in his life has already been shown. It remains now to tell the story of how he obtained his "woods".

When the Admiral dying in 1670 left William fifteen hundred pounds a year in rents from his estates, he also left him to collect if he could sixteen thousand pounds owing him by the Crown. This debt was for unpaid salary, money advanced by the Admiral and accumulated interest. In 1681 over ten years had elapsed and no payment had been made. Much as Charles II was beholden to the Admiral for his notable services in the Navy, he had too much else to do with his money to pay off such a large sum. From his standpoint it was better to "let sleeping dogs lie".

Now it will be remembered that Penn wrote to some of his friends a private letter which we have and in which he made a remark which has not attracted the attention it deserves. He said, in speaking of the sixteen thousand pounds of his estate, "that had I not been what I am I had long ago obtained."[38] What does this cryptic remark mean? Does it mean that if he had not been a Quaker, he would long ago have pressed the King for a discharge of the debt? Or does it mean that if he had not belonged to a despised and hated religious sect, the King would long ago have paid him? The question cannot be answered now. Nor do we know what motive prompted him to take up the subject in his petition to the King in June, 1680. It may be as some have thought that he needed money for his scale of living at the time. But with his wife's money added to his own, he had enough to take care of his family and to spend liberally in the interests of his co-religionists. Moreover, if he needed ready money, he knew he would not get it by this petition for a grant of land. On the contrary, it was bound to involve him in new expense. We must look for a more altruistic motive.

This may be found in the interest he had developed in the British possessions beyond seas, and this interest was connected with his passionate concern to promote religious toleration. He had already during the past thirteen years written numerous treatises and spoken much in furtherance of this concern. He had reminded his people that "force never yet made a good Christian or a good subject;"[39] "nothing can be more unreasonable than to compel men to believe against their belief, or to trouble them for practising what they believe, when it thwarts not the moral law of God;"[40] and he asks "what more unchristian than to use external force to sway the conscience of men about the exercise of religious worship?"[41]

Such pertinent comments and questions were aroused by the application of the Conventicle Act forbidding the assembly of more than five adults for religious worship except in Anglican churches, by the law requiring oaths of allegiance and supremacy though against the conscience, and by the law requiring all to pay tithes for the maintenance of the Establishment. As none of these laws was applicable in the famous trial of Penn and Mead in 1670 for street preaching in London, the two men were charged with causing a riot, and after a farcical trial were sentenced to Newgate along with the jury whose verdict had not satisfied the court! A blow by blow account of this trial which, after review by the court of common pleas, established the right of juries to bring in a verdict in accordance with their conscience, has been lately reprinted and is easily accessible. It showed Penn's spirit and legal acumen at the age of twenty-six. Thereafter he had plenty of personal reasons to carry toleration constantly in his mind.

It must not be supposed that William Penn and his Friends descended upon America out of a clear sky. The Quakers had been interested in America for over twenty-five years. First to Boston, later through the wilderness from Virginia to Massachusetts they had been doing missionary work on foot and on horseback, and to certain islands of the West Indies men and women had sailed "to preach the everlasting gospel." For the sake of these missionaries and early Quaker colonists, Friends in England had been urged as early as 1658 to "liberally offer up our earthly substance, according as God hath blessed every one."[42] George Fox included in many of his epistles encouragement and instructions for Quakers who had settled in Virginia, Carolina, Maryland and New England. There had even been plans for a Quaker community on the Susquehanna, but the plans fell through. The Friends in England were decidedly America-minded for years before Penn had the opportunity to carry out his "holy experiment."

In a very interesting letter to his friend Robert Turner in 1681, Penn states that he "had an opening of joy as to these parts [Pennsylvania] in the year 1661, at Oxford, twenty years since."[43] An "opening" is a Quaker expression to this day, signifying a "divine revelation" or "intimation of importance". It is possible that in 1661 as a seventeen-year-old boy he had nothing more than an intelligent interest in lands that his countrymen were so rapidly taking up and about which romantic descriptions were current. Perhaps there would be established there a more substantial Utopia than those proposed in the paper dreams of Plato, More or James Harrington. It is possible, however, with his early experience with intolerance and persecution even at Oxford, that his thoughts already ran out to a continent where religious toleration might be established. In 1677 as a young married man, Penn received a visit from three travelling preachers, of whom Fox himself was one, from whom he could learn of the colonies they had seen and of the conditions there. It is possible they gave details with the express purpose of enlisting the cooperation of this rich young man.

At about the same time Penn became fortuitously involved in the affairs of New Jersey. He with two other trustees was appointed to administer the interests of one Byllinge and one Fenwick, both Quakers to whom Lord Berkeley had sold his grant of West New Jersey from the Duke of York ten years earlier. The details of the transaction need not be recounted, but the result was that Penn as the principal trustee drew up a constitution known as "The Concessions and Agreements of the Proprietors, Freeholders and Inhabitants of West New Jersey in America". Nowhere else in all the world could there be found such a liberal religious spirit. Neither the great charter of Virginia nor the Mayflower compact is comparable in liberality, tolerance and the protection of individual rights.

Penn did not mistake the historical importance of this document. Speaking of it, he said in a letter of 1676 to Richard Hartshorne: "There we lay a foundation for after ages to understand

their liberty as men and Christians, that they may
not be brought in bondage, but by their own consent; for we put the power in the people, that is to
say, they to meet and choose one honest man for
each propriety who hath subscribed the concessions; all these men to meet as an assembly,
there to make and repeal laws, to choose a
governor, or a commissioner, and twelve assis-
tants to execute the laws during their pleasure;
so every man is capable to choose or to be
chosen. No man to be arrested, condemned,
imprisoned or molested in his estate or liberty
but by twelve men of the neighborhood; no
man to lie in prison for debt, but that his estate
satisfy as far as it will go, and he be set at liberty
to work; no person to be called in question or
molested for his conscience, or for worshipping
according to his conscience; with many more
things mentioned in the said concessions."[44]
Only one who knows the state of civil oppression and religious persecution in England at the
time can fully appreciate the historical significance of such words. As Bancroft observes,
Penn "dared to cherish the noble idea of man's
capacity for self-government and right to it."[45]

It is necessary to have touched lightly upon
these beginnings of New Jersey for two reasons:
first, the business involved him directly for the
first time in the creation of an ideal commonwealth in America and doubtless whetted his
appetite for still greater freedom of control than
he could exercise as only one of several trustees;
second, the Concessions of 1676 antedate similar
liberal provisions for Pennsylvania by five years.
The "Holy Experiment" thus came near to
being performed in New Jersey. But, as has
been suggested, Penn's hands were not quite
free in the lands east of the Delaware. Like
Maryland, New Jersey was at first a proprietary
colony, but several other proprietors were involved. Though Penn did not visit New Jersey
at the time, he had property interests there and
must have thought quite continuously of America
from 1676 onward. When he was in Holland
and western Germany in 1677 with three other
prominent Friends, he had a chance to learn
of many pietistic and dissenting groups there
who were under persecution and who were ripe
for the suggestion of American colonization.
We see, then, how a combination of circum-

stances focussed Penn's interest upon America.
For the rest of his active life his mind was on
it, though he was prevented from spending more
than four years in his beloved "woods". The
condition of the growing Quaker population
in England was at its worst during the 1670s.
There was evidently a constituency there and
on the Continent which would be interested in
an asylum beyond the seas where religious freedom from persecution would be provided. It
was under these conditions that Penn bethought
him of an appeal to the King for the grant of
such a suitable territory.

It will be appropriate now to observe the
effect of these new and unexpected responsibilities of foreign colonization upon the character
and attitude of a young and zealous Quaker. It is
not easy after three hundred years to recapture
the personality of such a many-sided man as
William Penn. He had so many sides that it is
hard to see all around him and to be sure that
something has not escaped us. However, if we
are to warm up that bronze statue which is so
familiar to Philadelphians, we must think of
the Founder as a man of flesh and blood. It is

not that there is any lack of evidence from which we may reconstruct the man in his maturity, for few men have left such frank and open expressions of their feelings and sentiments as he. He wore his heart upon his sleeve. The difficulty is rather that there is so much evidence, and sometimes of a contradictory character.

Penn's life divides itself roughly into two periods, before and after his occupation with America. The two periods are about equal in duration. But it must be emphasized that he was always an Englishman and acted and thought as such. His training and point of view were that of a country-gentleman whose formative years were passed in a Puritan atmosphere. This fact unfitted him for participation in the more frivolous society of the Restoration. At one of his trials in 1671 he publicly challenged "all men, women and children upon earth, justly to accuse me of ever having seen me drunk, heard me swear, utter a curse, or speak one obscene word, (much less that I ever made it my practice)."[46] And this was after his sojourn of nearly two years in France, and after his share in the life of the vice-regal court of the

Duke of Ormond at Dublin. We may be sure
that at the age of twenty-seven Penn felt that
he had always conducted himself as a gentleman·

But serious as he was, Penn was no figure of
gloom. He was by nature affable, cheerful,
emotional, expansive and enthusiastic in his
approach to people and to new ideas. Even at
the close of his life, in a memorial document
drawn up by his Friends, he was described as
having been "as free from rigid gravity as he
was clear of unseemly levity."[47] That he preserved the friendship and good will of so many
men of the world after he had become a Quaker
is a tribute to his engaging social qualities and
integrity of character. There is much to indicate
that he would have cut a fine figure at the court
of the Stuarts, had he not disqualified himself
from all public preferment by becoming a
Quaker. Known to the world of the time as
"Mr. Penn", to his intimate friends he was
"Will Penn".

Surviving letters and other documents reveal
Penn as a loving and devoted husband. As a
father, he was deeply concerned for the moral
and religious development of his numerous

children. His admonitions and advices to his first wife and their three surviving children in 1682 have come down to us. These documents breathe deep affection and a desire to inculcate a sense of their future responsibilities. Unhappily, he was doomed to disappointment in the later fate of these three children. The eldest and most promising, his father's heir apparent, was named Springett and died at the age of nineteen. His daughter Letitia, whom he affectionately called "Tishe", by her later marriage with William Aubrey joined her husband in quite insistent demands for financial returns from Pennsylvania. The youngest child, William Jr. or "Billy", married early, had children whose descendants have survived, but turned out to be a wastrel and given to drink. Billy's conduct both in America for a short and in England for a much longer time broke his father's heart. We can read about that in Penn's confidential letters to James Logan. Family property in England and Ireland was entailed to William Penn Jr. and of it his father could not dispose.

The children of Penn's second marriage to Hannah Callowhill of Bristol did not reach maturity before their father's death. They inherited in America and of course during the eighteenth century greatly profited financially, though for the most part resident in England. Descendants of both marriages later associated with the Anglican church, against which in his early days Penn had directed such diatribes for its alleged intolerance. The failure of Penn to make Quakerism permanently attractive to those of his own household would have been a grievous disappointment. He certainly tried hard enough, perhaps too hard. His two wives remained faithful to the Society of Friends until their respective deaths in 1694 and 1728.

There can be no doubt that Penn's natural exuberance of temperament and peace of mind began to be adversely affected soon after he became financially involved in Pennsylvania. At that time he was just midway in his life-span of seventy-four years. Hitherto he had known persecution and imprisonment for his new faith; but he was happily married, with promising little children, a noble fortune, and with time to write and preach in accordance with his Quaker beliefs. Much of his written work between 1667

and 1682 is of a religious and diputatious nature
and does not concern us here.

But before going to America in 1682 he had
given repeated and eloquent expression to his
demand for liberty of conscience, freedom of
worship, exemption from legal oaths, and for
the right of trial by a jury of one's peers of the
neighborhood. These demands stem from the
Quaker belief in the sacredness of the individual
conscience, and from Penn's determination to
recapture the civil rights of all Englishmen
guaranteed centuries earlier by Magna Charta.
Later all these liberties were guaranteed by
Penn himself in his frames of government and
passed over into the constitution of the United
States.

So persistently was the idea of "liberty" in
the mind of Penn as a young man that we find
the word incorporated specifically in four of his
pamphlets between 1670 and 1681. The significant
titles of these works are *The People's Ancient and
Just Liberties Asserted* (1670), which is the account
of his trial at the Old Bailey in that year; *The
Great Case of Liberty of Conscience* (1671) partially
written in Newgate prison, which contains a

plea for a return to the "good old admirable laws of England", and in which he asserts that "force never yet made a good Christian or a good subject"; *Christian Liberty* (1674), a brief but pregnant development of the thesis that "nothing can be more unreasonable than to compel men to believe against their belief, or to trouble them for practicing what they believe, when it thwarts not the moral law of God"; *A Brief Examination and State of Liberty Spiritual* (1681), addressed particularly to Friends, pleading that unity in essentials is not threatened by variety in non-essentials.

The sum of all Penn's writings in favor of religious toleration and of individual rights is as follows:

1. Religion belongs outside the control of the state.

2. The civil rights of Englishmen must be regained.

3. The political union of loyal citizens does not depend upon unity of religious belief. Rather will loyalty and prosperity be increased, as in Holland, by granting religious toleration.

When we speak today of liberty, we think

CHARLES II.
Roy de la grande Bretagne

Vander Werff pinxit.   Petr. Drevet sculpsit.

of the Liberty Bell and the incidents of 1776,—a
period one hundred years later than the documents just mentioned. We think of freedom from
the oppression and injuries inflicted by the
government of George III,—the political independence of the Colonies from the mother-
country. But we should recall that the assertion
of this political liberty only came, and could
only come, after the acknowledgement of certain individual rights by a government in England
finally influenced by such men as William Penn.
Penn himself had no thought of questioning the
sovereignty of the British Crown. What he
sought was the choice of such good and just
men in Parliament as would make and observe
laws consistent with the rights of all Englishmen.
As stated at the outset, democratic progress in
modern times does not come until after religious
toleration has been secured. The American
Revolution of 1776 could not come until after
the English revolution of 1688 had broken
tyranny over men's minds. It took nearly a
century for religious toleration to ripen into the
declaration of an independent republic. Penn,
we may be sure, would be interested in the

Liberty Bell. We should have to tell him that
it was he more than anyone else who, however
unconsciously, had prepared the way for American independence.

As we look back, it was a formidable enterprise which the wealthy young Quaker assumed
in 1681. Full of hope and buoyed up by the participation of the original purchasers, his activity
knew no bounds and his expenses were endless.
All the cost of legal transactions, of setting up
and maintaining the proprietary interests through
representatives and deputies in Pennsylvania fell
upon him personally. Transportation, extensive
surveys and his building projects in the province
were added to the normal cost of residence and
support for his family in England. All the fortune
he poured into Pennsylvania he expected to get
back in the form of quit-rents for land sold.
These rents were very small but should have
been very numerous as sales in the back-country
increased. The expectation of their adequacy
was never realized by the Founder. Costs of
government were always greater than income
from sales of land. In a generous spirit he de-
clined a share in the customs of Philadelphia

when it was offered him, but he came later to regret his generosity. Advantage was taken of his absence in England to withhold support to which he was entitled. The Penn-Logan correspondence leaves no doubt as to the financial clouds which were gathering during a quarter of a century around the too trusting and genial Penn. As late as 1704 he wrote to Logan: "Oh Pennsylvania, what hast thou not cost me! Above 30,000 pounds more than I ever got by it."[48]

He had opponents too. Some of the Anglican party after 1702 were relentless in their attempts to undermine Penn at court and to bring about the end of his governorship. Some of his own Friends at home also were made to fear by reports from Pennsylvania that their distinguished fellow-member had stepped out of his class and had overreached himself. The latter critics Penn could effectively take care of in his own way; but the anti-Proprietary party in Philadelphia made such trouble that Penn had considered as early as 1702 selling the government, but not his proprietary interests, to the Crown for 12,000 pounds. Only the illness in 1712 which rendered any legal action impossible on his part prevented the consummation of this sale.

In recalling these facts we are thinking of their effect upon Penn's character and personality. Sharing enthusiastically in all the principles of Quakerism, he found himself at the age of thirty-seven the promoter of an enterprise and the personal proprietor of a province so vast and so distant as to be beyond the dreams of any Quaker of the time. Penn was in a class by himself. Quaker practice was not originally developed for a man in such a position. There would be times when either he or his faith would have to "give". There were such times, and the tragedy for Penn lay in his knowledge of the fact.

Had it not been for Pennsylvania, Penn might have been a "plain" Friend, like some of his intimate associates; as it was, his circumstances and responsibilities made it impossible for him to be so. He was not only *in* the world; he was also *of* it. He meant for his life to accord perfectly with his profession as set forth in many of his writings. But actually worry over family matters and growing financial embarrassment distracted a spirit which he would fain have devoted to higher interests.

One does not like to think of this lover of liberty being in confinement himself for debt. Yet in 1708 Penn voluntarily sought refuge for eleven months in the precincts of the Fleet debtors' prison. We have seen the Founder elevated to heights of exultant joy during his first visit to Pennsylvania. By 1708 he had run the gamut of human emotions and was now prostrated in chagrin. He was the victim of his own carelessness rather than guilty of any evil intention. For years Philip Ford had been his financial steward from whom he had borrowed money for his large undertakings. Having carelessly signed certain documents, he found himself sued by the heirs of Ford for the extravagant sum of 14,000 pounds. It was for some months while his friends compounded this debt and raised the funds to discharge it for 6,800 pounds that Penn remained in the Fleet.

His lack of financial care and his failure to judge wisely of human character were Penn's two shortcomings. Time and again he selected men for important posts who were incompetent. His easy-going attitude as a spender was incon-

sistent with the difficulty he had in securing his
income. A man who sees his assets dwindling
has many bad moments. As the head of a growing family he was plainly worried for the future.
Family property in England and Ireland having
been entailed to his eldest surviving son, Penn
had no hope of reviving his own fortune but by
sales of land in Pennsylvania. His state of concern
is plainly revealed in the irritation and chagrin
manifested in his letters to Logan. Here we have
what we meant by the conflict between his Quaker
calm and the anxious situation in which he found
himself for many years. This agony of soul has
not been sufficiently stressed by his biographers.
It set him apart from all other Quakers of his
day. When he wrote from London to Logan in
1705 "I am a crucified man between Injustice
and Ingratitude there, and Extortion and Oppression here", he was using language which
could not be matched in Quaker literature.[49]

The Society of Friends in the seventeenth
century furnishes no example of a man who had
such problems laid upon a tender conscience. No
other Quaker had so much at stake. Not only
was the financial situation acute. Another respon-

sibility weighed upon him: this was his personal duty to the colonists who had confided their future to him in a promised land. Logan estimated in 1702 that though Friends were more numerous in the country, the population of Philadelphia was already about two-thirds non-Quaker.[50] This fact threatened the very conditions which had made Philadelphia originally a Quaker town, and Penn was only too well reminded of the fact. He saw no remedy for the situation but to sell his government, and upon advice given him was fully prepared to do so soon after his final return to England.

In the seventeenth century, to be a consistent Quaker was recognized to be a full-time job. Quakers were then perfectionists, and to be perfect requires all of one's time and attention. This is so true that early Quaker biographies pass over the details of daily life with complete indifference. In memoirs which are primarily records of spiritual struggles we can learn almost nothing about the impact of daily reality upon the individual. Penn bid fair to be no exception to this general rule. We know very little of the twenty-three years which preceded his conver-

sion to Quakerism, because in his estimation
that was when his true life began. It is significant
that, when he related for some friends in Germany an account of his own life and experiences,
he passed over the events of twenty-three years
in a single paragraph of twenty lines.[51]

But soon after his conversion Penn became
immersed in many affairs beside purely personal
struggles with the devil. Circumstances com-
bined to make him feel that he was a chosen
disciple. Birth, wealth, education and worldly
connections set him apart. It was his period of
combative preaching, debating and writing on
behalf of his new-found faith. He was afraid
of no one and nothing. He wrote from the Tower
"my prison shall be my grave before I will
budge a jot; for I owe my conscience to no
mortal man."[52] This was in 1669. A year later,
when sentenced this time to Newgate, he boldly
told the Lieutenant of the Tower, Sir John
Robinson: "I would have thee and all other men
know that I scorn that religion which is not
worth suffering for, and able to sustain those
that are afflicted for it."[53] The polemical treatises
of these ten years are full of an uncompromising

dedication to the Quaker way of life as then
held and practiced.

With this dedication we note the determination
to secure again for Englishmen the legal and
property rights guaranteed by Magna Charta.
Better treatment of his co-religionists was con-
tingent upon the restoration of these ancient
rights and liberties. As he wrote to the Judges
of Middlesex: "There can be no reason to per-
secute any man in this world about any thing
that belongs to the next."[54] Throughout his life
he held to the conviction that the state had no
rights over conscience and that the state was
most safe and prosperous when it made no effort
to force the established church upon all citizens.
The continuous preaching and writing of Penn
made him by 1681 a man of mark. He was justified
in writing to the Indians in that year, deploring
the manner in which they had been treated by
some, "I am not such a man, as is well known
in my own country."[55]

Penn's religious enthusiasm and good humor
continued throughout the early negotiations concerning New Jersey and Pennsylvania. He felt
sure of himself and of his right guidance. He

rejoiced that he was now in a position to settle
a government which should be free from mischiefs. His most notable pronouncements regarding government date from this time. He
determined for himself to keep hands off, in
order that "the will of one man may not hinder
the good of an whole country."[56] The same year
he wrote to his steward James Harrison: " 'Tis
a good country, with a good conscience it will
do well. I am satisfied in it, and leave it with
the Lord."[57]

After seeing his new country for himself, his
satisfaction with its material promise was un-
abated. To one correspondent he wrote: "In
fine, here is what an Abraham, Isaac and Jacob
would be well contented with; and service
enough for God, for the fields are here white for
harvest. O, how sweet is the quiet of these parts,
freed from the anxious and troublesome solicita-
tions, hurries, and perplexities of woeful
Europe!"[58] To the Free Society of Traders, in
which he was himself a shareholder, he wrote at
length a glowing description of the natural
resources of his province and of its primitive
inhabitants. To the noble friend of his youth,

the Earl of Sunderland, he boasted "that by the help of God and such noble friends I will show a province in seven years equal to her neighbours of forty years planting."[59] And to the Marquess of Halifax he writes with frank satisfaction: "I have lead the greatest colony into America that ever any man did upon a private credit, and the most prosperous beginnings that ever were in it, are to be found among us."[60]

These words were written in the heyday of his adventure. The future was full of promise, his first colonists trusted him, he was confident that God was with him. Penn's early biographers have all dwelt lovingly upon the rich land which he entered in person in 1682, the good will of its earlier European inhabitants, his just treatment of the Indians who have regarded his Quaker descendants ever since as their friends and protectors: here would be a Utopia where peace, mercy, justice and plenty should prevail in a heaven-directed democracy.

But already there is a hint of anxiety. In the letter to Halifax just quoted he expresses his fear about the rival claims of Lord Baltimore to the shores of Delaware Bay: if anything were to threaten Penn's approach to the sea, he says "my voyage will be a ruinous one to me and my partners, which God defend." It was indeed the claim of Lord Baltimore affecting the southern boundary of Pennsylvania that took Penn back to England in 1684. His colonial honeymoon was over. From the congenial pursuits of laying out manors, conferring with the Indians, presiding at courts and councils, riding through the forest and preaching at meetings, he returned to the haggling negotiations and constant pleadings of old-world London. How familiar are his emotions to some Americans in our own day! There is a touching nostalgia in his parting "prayer for Philadelphia" contained in an open letter to the members of his religious Society in the little city. A subtle fear as well as faith and hope is felt in the words:

"And thou Philadelphia, the virgin settlement of this province, named before thou wert born, what love, what care, what service, and what travail has there been to bring thee forth and preserve thee from such as would abuse and defile thee!

"O that thou mayest be kept from the evil

that would overwhelm thee: that, faithful to the God of thy mercies, in the life of righteousness, thou mayest be preserved to the end!"[61]

As stated elsewhere, there can be no doubt that soon after his first return to England Penn's worldly burdens seriously interfered with his spiritual serenity. These burdens and responsibilities, financial and administrative, were such as no "plain" Friend ever had to bear. "Plain" Friends, like the early Publishers of Truth, travelled light. Many of them possessed little here below beside what they stood up in. They eschewed what John Woolman later called the "cumber" of this world. Whether they worked in their homes or in prison, their spiritual life flowed on without interruption and without the least weakening. But Penn's case was different. Stephen Crisp, one of his most intimate and respected friends, wrote to him while he was still on his first visit to Philadelphia: "I have had a sense of the various spirits, and intricate cases, and multiplicity of affairs, and these of various kinds, which daily attend thee, enough to drink up thy spirit, and tire thy soul; and which if it be not kept to the inexhaustible Fountain, may

be dried up. And this I must tell thee, which
thou also knowest, that the highest capacity of
natural wit and parts will not, and cannot,
perform what thou hast to do, namely, to propa-
gate and advance the interest and profit of Government and Plantation, and at the same time to
give the interest of Truth and testimony of the
holy name of God their due preference in all
things."62

Stephen Crisp saw how his friend was involved. For Penn, with all his intentions, never
quite got free from the world into which he had
been born. He had inherited some worldly
obligations; he had assumed in middle age far
greater burdens. He had a duty to many people
who looked to him for their support and defense.
For many years he was the titled suppliant at
court for Friends and others in distress. His
financial obligations became more and more
involved after 1682. His relations to the Crown
as a feudal proprietor were at odds with his
desires for the privileges he had guaranteed to
his colonists in Pennsylvania. The requirement
of legal oaths was constantly urged by the church
party, to the disruption of justice through

absenteeism, disqualification of judges and the nullification of evidence in court procedure. Scarcity of ready money and the interruption of sea-borne trade due to the incessant wars with France from 1689 to 1713 made the collection of rents almost impossible. Loss or capture of cargoes in which he had a share straitened him. The dissatisfaction of the "Lower Counties", New Castle, Sussex and Kent with their relations to the three Pennsylvania counties of Philadelphia, Chester and Bucks was a source of constant irritation to the Proprietor until their final separation as the future State of Delaware in 1703. The schism in Quakerism fomented by his old friend George Keith pained Penn. Succeeding deputy-governors were unpopular; some of them died, others retired in discomfiture. Lord Baltimore carried on a continuous lobby in London in the interests of Maryland against Pennsylvania. It was alleged by the anti-proprietary party that the Quakers failed to proceed against piracy in Delaware Bay, that the British navigation laws were not observed, and that the Quaker-controlled Assembly refused grants for the military purposes of the colonies. Disturbing reports of these matters were forwarded to the colonial authorities in England and kept Penn constantly in hot water in London and troubled his secretary after 1702 in Philadelphia. Such a summary enumeration reveals that Penn had no pathway of roses for thirty years of active association with Pennsylvania affairs.

As a result of representations made by the hostile anti-proprietary party, Penn's government was taken from him in 1692. Just at this time the Founder was harried by the accusation that he was a Jesuit in disguise and that he had treacherously corresponded with James II since his flight. Supported by old and influential friends at court, Penn was able to refute such absurd charges, and the restoration of his government by King William in 1694 ensued. Thus Penn was in trouble whichever way he looked. When in London he wished to be in Pennsylvania; when in Pennsylvania his presence was required in London. And it took many months sometimes to exchange dispatches between the two foci of his interests.

Nor were the griefs of his private life any less

Place before this Reign.

JAMES THE SECOND, KING OF ENGLAND, SCOTLAND, FRANCE AND IRELAND &c.

DIEU ET MON DROIT

G. Kneller pinxit.

R. Sheppard Sculp!

poignant toward the end of the century. While he was under the royal displeasure he retired from public life entirely, using the enforced leisure to publish his *Fruits of Solitude* (1693), the best known of his works to posterity, and also his *Essay towards the Present and Future Peace of Europe* (1693), a paper which still deserves study by those interested in a union of the world Powers for peace. Soon after his emergence from obscurity Penn's beloved wife died in 1694. Shortly after his second marriage in 1696 to the mature and competent Hannah Callowhill of Bristol, he lost his eldest son Springett upon whom his hopes had been set. His next son, William Jr., married early and had children who later became a joy to their aging grandfather; but the son himself, given to drink and gay company as has been said, was only a source of shame and expense to his father. In the midst of his family troubles, and under the threatened resignation of their powers by the Proprietors of New Jersey, Penn wrote to Logan in 1701: "Let's do our duty, and leave the rest with God."[63] That sums up his Quaker philosophy as a man of the world.

The tragedy of Penn's personal life has not been hitherto sufficiently stressed. His advanced ideas have been so universally hailed, the eventual prosperity of his province has been so convincingly witnessed, that the disappointment of his own hopes and ambitions for it and for his family have been overlooked. From the financial distress and from the bickerings of colonists he was perhaps mercifully delivered by six years of a second childhood from 1712 to 1718 when none of these things could reach him. Yet, as Bancroft said, "his name is now wide as the world; he is one of the few who have gained abiding glory,"[64] because of the people's liberties which he championed. These liberties must now claim our attention.

IV

THE days for the creation of Proprietary governments in British colonies were well-nigh past, and the imperial policy of the eighteenth century was already foreshadowed in 1680 when Penn made his appeal to Charles II. He was the last to receive such a grant in America. Certainly no other Quaker could have asked for such a grant, and probably no other Quaker could have financed it. So, in a different sense from Napoleon, Penn was a "man of destiny". Both Charles II and the Duke of York must have been singularly favorable to Penn, or he would not have been successful in the face of

opposition offered by those who favored establishment in the future of Crown colonies only.

But, though Penn would not have called it
by such a name, he had what is popularly called
"an ace up his sleeve". We do not know if he
had to lay the card on the table, or whether
Charles and his Privy Council remembered the
16,000 pound debt only too well and did not
need to be reminded of it. The application
having been made in 1680, the charter after
considerable difficulty was signed on March 4,
1681 and formally proclaimed the following April
2. A copy is in Harrisburg. Thus the royal debt
was cancelled by the grant to Penn as Proprietor
and Governor of a territory he had never seen,
lying between Maryland and New York west
of the Delaware River, and which included for
nearly twenty-five years the three "lower counties" now forming the State of Delaware, added
to Penn's original grant through the good will
of the Duke of York.

Early in 1704 these three lower counties
withdrew from the jurisdiction of Pennsylvania,
though sharing until the Revolution the same
governor. It will thus be seen that New Jersey,

Pennsylvania and Delaware are the three States which benefited directly by Penn's provision for their future citizens. It is interesting that these three colonies were the first to ratify the constitution in December 1787.

In this place it will be appropriate to observe how the Crown safeguarded certain of its prerogatives in the original charter, and then to consider the liberal provisions for his colonists in Penn's early frames and constitutions.

First, the King's charter states that the territory specified is confirmed to William Penn and his heirs forever to enlarge the empire and its interests and "to reduce the savage natives by gentle and just manners to the love of civil society and Christian religion."[65] The outright grant of the land and "certain privileges and jurisdictions requisite for the good government and safety of the said country and colony" may be regarded as discharging the royal debt of sixteen thousand pounds. This ownership of the soil by the Penns could not be taken away from them, but the governorship could be, and later was temporarily taken from William Penn between 1692 and 1694. New Jersey similarly was made a Crown colony finally in 1702, and the Calverts in Maryland were deprived of their governorship from 1691 to 1716.

Important points in the twenty-three sections of the charter of Charles II are as follows:

1. The grant is made having regard to the divers services of the petitioner's father, Admiral Sir William Penn. The bounds of the grant are specified.

2. The privilege is granted the proprietor of establishing ports, of enjoying fishing rights and exploiting mines.

3. The territory is to be holden of the kings of England in free and common socage, by fealty only for all services, and not in capite or by knights service; two beaver skins annually to be delivered at Windsor, and one-fifth of all gold and silver found; the name to be Pensilvania.

4. Power to appoint deputies, publish laws, raise money for public use etc. with the assent and approval of the freemen of the country or their delegates.

5. Authority to appoint Justices and other public administrative officers; to try all crimes except treason and murder, the latter to be

reprieved until the royal pleasure be known therein. All laws to be "consonant to reason" and agreeable to the laws of England, with the right of appeal from any judgment in Pennsylvania to the courts of England.

6. English law protecting all persons to prevail until and unless new ordinances for the preservation of peace be made by the proprietors and freemen consonant with the laws of England.

7. To prevent any departure from the faith and allegiance due to the Law of England, all laws passed in Pennsylvania shall be within five months transmitted to the Privy Council for approval within six months; if then found to be inconsistent with royal sovereignty or lawful prerogative, they shall be declared void.

8. Permission for British subjects to colonize and provision themselves, paying only the customs due.

9. License to trade and transport produce and merchandise upon payment of all duties and impositions now or in the future declared to be legal.

10. To divide the country, incorporate towns and establish such markets etc. as may be convenient.

11. Under English laws of navigation which were to be enforced, cargoes may be sent to English ports only, and then within one year transshipped if desired to foreign destinations. [Alleged violations in Pennsylvania of the navigation laws were an early cause of embarrassment between Penn and the Crown.]

12. Certain ports to be designated in Pennsylvania for lading and unlading ships, these ports to admit and receive commissioners of the royal customs.

13. After satisfaction of the royal customs under act of Parliament, Penn and his heirs may enjoy such customs as may be established by themselves and the people in representative assembly.

14. An attorney or agent to be appointed by Penn in London to answer in his behalf for any misdemeanors, default, or neglect of the laws of navigation. If penalties and satisfaction are not forthcoming within one year, "Then it shall be lawful for us . . . to seize and resume the government of the said province . . ., and the same to retain until payment shall be made thereof. But notwithstanding any such seizure

or resumption of the government, nothing concerning the propriety or ownership of any lands
etc. of the adventurers, planters or owners . . .
shall be any way affected or molested thereby."
[This important article thus guarantees the
permanent ownership but not the governorship
of Penn and his heirs or assigns.]

15. No correspondence allowed with enemies
of England, and no hostile action toward any
people in league or amity with England.

16. Penn empowered to levy and train citizens
to pursue and war upon enemies and robbers by
sea or land within or without the province, to
put them to death or save them as is the prerogative of any Captain General of an army.

17. The right to sell or lease under any conditions parcels of land, "as of the seignory of
Windsor," by such service, customs and rents
as Penn may determine, "and not immediately
of us, our heirs and successors." [Thus Penn's
future purchasers held their land directly from
him, as he in turn held Pennsylvania from the
king through the annual payment at Windsor
of two beaver skins. This essentially feudal
arrangement is important.]

18. Further development of 17.

19. Permission to erect manors and to hold courts baron under license of Penn.

20. No taxes or customs to be set or made in future except with the consent of the Governor and Assembly or by Act of Parliament in England. [Before the Revolution this last clause became significant.]

21. All royal courts and judges are enjoined to do nothing contrary to the preceding articles, but "be at all times aiding and assisting as is fitting unto the said William Penn . . . in the full use and fruition of the benefit of this our charter."

22. Provision for an Anglican preacher, upon request of twenty petitioners to the Bishop of London, to be received and to reside "without any denial or molestation whatsoever."

23. Unless due allegiance to the Crown be threatened, the royal courts are enjoined so to interpret this charter at all times "as shall be adjudged most advantageous and favorable unto the said William Penn, his heirs and assigns."

The scene when the royal signature was affixed to this document must have caused a thrill to Penn. He had just received what was to prove the most valuable grant ever made by England to a private individual. And, within the feudal relations stipulated by the Crown, he was free to establish such a government and laws as he personally might desire. What he desired is therefore of great significance for American institutions. Whereas Massachusetts and Connecticut intended to defend their theocratic oligarchy and to hold their line against all intruders of other faiths, Penn planned a theocratic democracy which should evolve through the popular will under divine guidance. The former looked backward, as did also the feudal aristocracy planned by Locke for Carolina, while Penn looked forward, and his political theory could be adopted by the future writers of the constitution. Perhaps Woodrow Wilson had this fact in mind when he told the New Jersey Historical Society: "The local history of the Middle States,—New York, New Jersey and Pennsylvania—is much more structurally a part of the characteristic life of the nation as a whole than is the history of the New England communities or of the several States and regions of the South."[66]

There were surely some present in 1681 who
disapproved the policy of granting a charter
for another proprietary colony. But the King
was in a good humor at having discharged a debt
at so little cost. Judging by his later generosity
with the three lower counties, the Duke of
York for his part could have manifested no
chagrin. To the principals, the transaction must
have seemed a good piece of business all around.
Penn himself was so delighted at the prospect
thus opened before him that he wrote at once
to his intimate friend Robert Turner in Ireland
an account of the "many waitings, watchings,
solicitings and disputes in council"[67] which were
terminated by the consummation of his hopes.
He tells how his own choice of a name was first
New Wales, and then Silvania. But as we have
seen, the King had inscribed Pensilvania. Fearing
that the name would be looked upon as a vanity
in him, "and not as a respect in the King, as it
truly was to my father whom he often mentions
with praise," Penn confesses that he offered the
Undersecretarys twenty guineas to vary the
name! But without success. The name was
irrevocable, and Pennsylvania is the only State

in the Union which incorporates the family name of its founder.

Penn lost no time in forwarding his design. Five weeks after receiving the charter he published a prospectus which had been submitted for the approval of "traders, planters and ship-masters, that know those parts," and of the most eminent Friends in London. In an accompanying letter to Robert Turner *et al* he says: "As my understanding and inclinations have been much directed to observe and reprove mischiefs in governments, so it is now put into my power to settle one. For the matters of liberty and privilege, I purpose that which is extraordinary, and to leave myself and successors no power of doing mischief."[68]

In this oft-quoted letter Penn confesses that he had long been interested in the theory of government and naturally rejoices in the opportunity to put his ideas into force. It has been seen what freedom in this respect was left to him by the royal charter. He was aware that the government he had in mind was extraordinary in that he renounced control by any one religious or aristocratic group. But in reality he had already provided for representative government in West New Jersey five years earlier. It requires an effort for us to realize the novelty in all this at a time when real democratic government through popular representation was unknown in Europe. So here in the western world a political philosopher for the first time in modern history had a free hand in creating the Utopia of which others had only dreamed.

Before Pennsylvania was founded Penn had expressed forcibly his ideas on the responsibility of his fellow-citizens for the integrity of their representatives in Parliament. Here are some sentiments which we still need to cherish: "There is nothing more your interest than for you to understand your right in the Government, and to be constantly jealous over it; for your well-being depends upon its preservation."[69] "No law can be made, no money levied, nor a penny legally demanded (even to defray the charge of the Government) without your consent."[70] "Every representative may be called the creature of this people, because the people make them, and to them they owe their being."[71] "Without the preservation of virtue it is impossible to

maintain the best constitution that can be made."[72]
And he pertinently reminded his own Council
in Pennsylvania in 1700: "Government is not
an end, but a means. He who thinks it to be an
end, aims at profit—to make a trade of it—but
he who thinks it to be a means, understands the
true end of government."[73]

During 1681 and 1682 numerous important
documents were issued by Penn testifying to his
absorption in plans for colonization and for
establishing a government in his new province.
The first of these is *Certain Conditions and Concessions* agreed upon in England by Penn and the
first purchasers of Pennsylvania lands. Of the
twenty articles comprised in this document, ten
concern land divisions and allotments and the
conditions attaching thereto; five treat of mis-
cellaneous matters; and no less than five bespeak
fair and just treatment of the Indians on the
same basis as white settlers.

It may be remarked here that the feature of
Penn's treatment of the natives is not that he
bought their lands with the trinkets they valued,
for that was done by other colonists and was
indeed commended to Penn as a policy by the

Bishop of London. The unique feature in Penn's case is his determination to approach the Indians as men and brothers and to maintain friendly relations with them. This is a principle which has distinguished the Quakers at all times in their relations with less privileged peoples. Throughout the Founder's life there was no deviation from this purpose, and the Indians' appreciation of his consideration has endured to the present time.

Lest any reader should remember the iniquitous "walking purchase", it should be pointed out that this deceptive trickery was practiced upon the Indians under the authority of Penn's son Thomas the Anglican governor in 1737 nearly twenty years after the Founder's death.

To the few settlers already on the Delaware Penn wrote that "it hath pleased God in his Providence to cast you within my lot and care. It is a business that, though I never undertook before, yet God has given me an understanding of my duty, and an honest mind to do it uprightly."[74] Here we find that profound sense of divine guidance which presided at the inception of the enterprise and which marks all

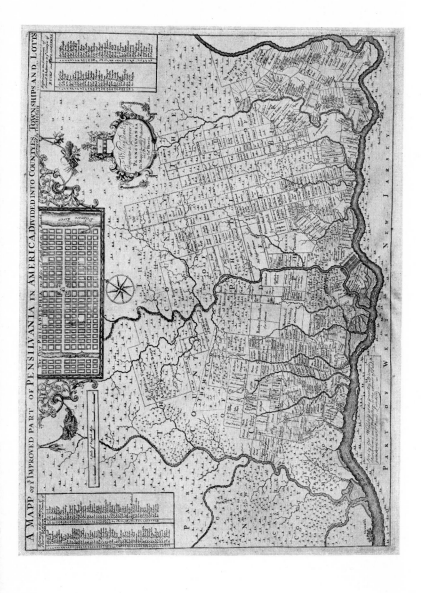

Penn's serious utterances regarding the responsibilities attaching to government.

Later in the summer he wrote to James Harrison: "For my country, I eyed the Lord in the
obtaining of it, and more was I drawn inward
to look to him and to owe it to his hand and
power, than to any other way. I have so obtained
it, and desire that I may not be unworthy of
his love, but do that which may answer his kind
providence, and serve his truth and people;
that an example may be set up to the nations;
there may be room there, though not here, for
such an holy experiment."[75] This is consistent
Quakerism applied, as it had never been applied
before, to the practical business of government.
It may be noted that Penn knew that a practical
illustration of good government would be more
effective than much preliminary talk. The experiment was a Quaker experiment, performed as a
demonstration before the eyes of Europe.

In the autumn of 1681 Penn dispatched three
commissioners to make preliminary surveys,
select the site for a town and block out the lots
for building purposes. One interesting result of
his instructions was the adoption of a checker-

board plan for Philadelphia streets, the numbered streets running north and south, and streets bearing the names of native trees running east and west. The checker-board plan had been recommended for the rebuilding of London after the great fire of 1666, but was not adopted. Many American cities have adopted the plan. But there is no city of Philadelphia's present size in the world in whose planning this feature was adopted so early as 1682.

The site chosen was the level neck of land lying between the Delaware and Schuylkill Rivers. This permitted an extensive water front-age for a considerable distance. Midway between the rivers at the intersection of High (Market) and Broad Streets was to be placed a ten-acre central square, now occupied by the City Hall, and spaced at intervals from it were the still existent squares now named for Washington, Franklin, Rittenhouse and Logan. The Founder proposed that the first houses should occupy the middle of their respective plots and thus leave room on either side for orchards and gardens, in order that it might be "a green country town" free from the fire hazard. He had reason to know what a great fire was like.

Given the factors in the making of William Penn which have already been mentioned, it is difficult not to see in his conception of religious duty applied to government the distinguishing feature in his case as a founder. Beside the rather conventional expressions for the christianizing of the natives, there were two motives which prompted English colonization in America. One was the extension of trade which interested the merchant class and their backers, the "gentlemen adventurers" at court who helped form the exploitation companies, secured the charters, put up the money, but seldom crossed the seas themselves. The other motive was the desire to secure religious freedom for some church group which was hampered or persecuted in England. It was in his reaction to the latter motive that Penn was remarkable.

As for other colonies, Massachusetts and Connecticut were founded by strong and determined religious groups. These colonies were to be religious commonwealths, founded upon a Calvinistic interpretation of the scriptures regarded as a final authority,—a closed revelation of the

divine will. They seem like American versions
of Calvin's Geneva, determined to preserve
their theocracy if necessary by violence, and
hostile to the intrusion of men of other faiths.
No religious tolerance is evident in their original
plans. There was no future for America in such
an outlook. Virginia, for its part, was an Anglican
preserve, Maryland an asylum for Roman Catholics. New York under both the Dutch and English
was quite frankly a trading-post for furs, and
little idealism is found in its early history.
Rhode Island, however, from the first had
petitioned for religious freedom and in the charter
of 1663 the principle was contained that no person in the colony should be molested or punished
or called in question for differences in matters
of religion, but should have full liberty in matters
of religious concernment, provided this liberty
be not used in licentiousness, civil injury or
outward disturbance of others. Massachusetts
and Connecticut Puritans and Manhattan Dutch
Reformed Calvinists all condemned this Rhode
Island expression of toleration, but the government of Charles II allowed it to pass despite
the persecution it was favoring at the time in the

home islands.

Of all the important seventeenth-century colonies, Maryland as conceived by George Calvert the first Lord Baltimore presents the greatest outward resemblance to Pennsylvania, both in its professed religious toleration, the fact that it was a grant to an individual proprietor, the later experience of the proprietary family and its nominal survival as a proprietary colony until the Revolution. Penn had one condition in his favor: his province was not founded until after the period of the Commonwealth, a period when the then existing colonies reflected in their governments the same heat of religious hatred and jealousy as existed for over ten years in England.

In Penn's mind religious toleration lay at the very root of his plan of colonization. It was not a new idea, but had already been incorporated in the constitutions of Maryland, Rhode Island and New Jersey. We have seen how after the Restoration in 1660 the subject was constantly agitated by publicists and by Penn himself. But the official progress of toleration had been painfully slow in the mother-country and also in

those existing colonies which reflected the attitude of Parliament on the question. However,
what *was* new in the Penn provinces was the
conception of a democratic government *evolving
under divine guidance*, the provision for refusal
to take or administer oaths either of allegiance
and supremacy or of a legal nature in courts of
law; so also, in another category, was the
legalization of marriage without the intermedi-
ation of priest or Justice of the Peace, and the
declaration of good will toward the Indians.

A minor effect of Quaker experience in
England is to be found in the many provisions
covering court-trials, juries, debtors, jails, fines
and penalties in Pennsylvania. Here Penn could
qualify as an expert, as also could many of his
early English and Welsh colonists. They had
been pointed out by paid informers, accused by
tithe-gatherers, tried without juries, sentenced
upon false evidence, confined in stinking jails
and foul dungeons for months and years, where
several hundred of them had died, and their
possessions, cattle, and tools had been distrained
and sold to satisfy the claims of avaricious
churchmen. The less the Quakers saw of courts

in the future, the better pleased they would be.

Indeed, in his letter of 1683 to the Committee of the Free Society of Traders, Penn reported that "there are three peacemakers chosen by every county court, in the nature of common arbitrators, to hear and end differences between man and man." Thus in personal affairs as in international relations, Friends had been warned by Fox to keep out of "janglings and parties" and "the bustlings of the world."[76] Arbitration is of the very essence of Quaker philosophy in the attempt to do justice. "A wise man will not give both his ears to one party, but reserve one for the other party, and will hear both, and then judge,"[77] said Fox. Even today the inquiry is made in Quaker Meetings: "Where differences arise, are prompt endeavors made to end them?" St. Paul's advice in I *Cor.* vi is still pertinent.

It is interesting to observe how Penn's early laws protected the defendant from the abuse and bullying with which he was himself all too familiar in English courts. He contributed to the element of mercy in our modern administration of justice, and provided for work to be done in individual cells instead of an idle existence in a promiscuous dungeon. This was long considered a great advance in the treatment of criminals. These reforms were the result of the Quaker belief in the inherent dignity and sacred character of the individual because of the spark of the divine in all men. On Penn as a law-giver Montesquieu remarked: "Mr. Penn is a real Lycurgus: and though the former made peace his aim, as the latter did war, yet they resemble one another in the singular way of living to which they reduced their people, in the ascendant they had over free men, in the prejudices they overcame, and in the passions which they subdued."[78]

Despite the long boundary dispute between the families of Penn and Calvert, their experience as colonial proprietors is very similar. The first Lord Baltimore tried an experiment in what has been called "a hazardous act of religious knight-errantry." Protestants were to be allowed to live in peace and amity with the Proprietor's Catholic followers. As the century progressed, they failed to do so.

So also Penn reminiscing in 1705 wrote: "I went thither [Pennsylvania] to lay the foundation of a free colony for all mankind, that should go thither, more especially those of my own persuasion; not that I would lessen the civil liberties of others because of their persuasion, but screen and defend our own from any infringement on that account."[79]

With the Catholic George Calvert the provision of toleration was perhaps a matter of policy in gaining his Charter; with Penn the Quaker it was the result of his humanitarian solicitude for all sufferers for conscience' sake in England and on the Continent. He was destined to have his hopes shattered after the arrival of many Anglicans and Scotch-Irish Presbyterians. But the principle was not violated, and the province came to be governed in mid-eighteenth century by a democratic majority of these very denominations in the Assembly.

It will be seen now that our reservations about the priority of Penn's provisions for toleration were warranted: Maryland and Rhode Island had both anticipated New Jersey and Pennsylvania. What distinguished Penn's early frames and constitutions between 1681 and 1701 was his personal solicitude over a continuous period that his government should be conducted in accordance with his religious principles. This solicitude has been called hopelessly idealistic, Quixotic and impractical. That point of view may of course be maintained, in view of certain failures and disappointments which thwarted the Founder's hopes. But Pennsylvania had become the most important colony before 1776, and Penn's principles are still there, hung high in air, for all to see and study. Where they have failed, it has been because of men's distrust of spiritual controls. It has yet to be proven that they are impractical when men are sufficiently advanced in civil society to embrace them. Penn believed always that a government based on Christian principles paid in terms of national contentment and prosperity. His great seal of 1699 bore the words *Mercy, Justice, Truth, Peace, Love, Plenty.*

In seeking to present William Penn in the proper light, it is well to recall certain facts at the time when he wrote his first constitutions. Born as he had been in the privileged class, with wealth and a good education, with influential and intelligent friends, he was by education and sympathy in 1681 a country-gentleman, an aristocrat. But he had become a Quaker in 1667, and

that fact leveled out in theory his social dis-
tinctions. It made of his colonial enterprise
primarily a religious concern, in which he also
hoped to be compensated for the huge invest-
ment he himself made in it, and to leave to his
children a fine patrimony for their heritage and
residence. Forms of government did not greatly
concern him as we shall see.

What *did* concern him and all Quakers was
that righteousness should be promoted among
the people, that virtue should be rewarded and
evil kept down. In theory, he was ready to
trust the people to pursue this objective, and
therein lay much of his originality. In practice,
he at first reserved a treble vote for himself or
his deputy in the Council, a touch of privilege
so unpopular that he speedily revoked that
provision. Again, when in Pennsylvania, he is
said to have insisted on certain recognition of
his position as governor. Though personally
modest, he believed in the prestige due to his
official position. But he did not retreat from the
position he had taken in 1676 in the letter already
quoted that "we put the power in the people."

Indeed, all the progress made between 1681

and 1701 was in the direction of more popular control. What Penn resented as a father of his people was not the assertion of democratic claims in the Assembly, but the ungrateful and arrogant tone assumed by some of its members in making claims upon their benefactor and in defrauding him of his legitimate income. When he was in the depths of disillusion regarding Pennsylvania politics in 1705, he wrote to Judge Mompesson: "There is an excess of vanity that is apt to creep in upon the people in power in America, who, having got out of the crowd in which they were lost here [in England], upon every little eminency there, think nothing taller than themselves but the trees, and as if there were no superior judgement to which they should be accountable; so that I have sometimes thought that if there was a law to oblige the people in power, in their respective colonies, to take turns in coming over for England, that they might lose themselves again amongst the crowds of so much more considerable people at the custom-house, exchange, and Westminster Hall, they would exceedingly amend in their conduct at their return, and be much more discreet and

tractable, and fit for government. In the mean
time, pray help to prevent them not to destroy
themselves."[80]

Penn was always an Englishman, and it is
amusing to see him longing to put the American
spokesmen in their place by treating them to a
little educational tour. He felt his colonists in
"the land of the free" had been a little too quick
to "feel their oats." As a gentleman himself,
he liked to see things done decently and in order,
and he felt that some of the leaders in Pennsylvania needed further education.

We have just anticipated a quarter of a century
and descried the troubles Penn had in adjusting
theory and practice, Quakerism and worldly
wisdom, feudal responsibility to the Crown with
fidelity to his colonists. We may go back now
and see how religion suffused every effort he
made to secure the wise government of his
province. It would be tedious to consider in
succession the First Frame and Laws Agreed
upon in England later incorporated in the Great
Law of 1682, the second Frame of 1683, the new
Frame required by circumstances in 1696 and
the Charter of Privileges of 1701 under which

Pennsylvania was governed until 1776. During all this time there was steady progress toward popular control at the expense of proprietary prerogatives. Practically Penn told his people to proceed and enact such laws as they agreed upon, provided they were consonant with the laws of England and fair to him as proprietor of the soil. He had no desire to control law-making. There was to be no proprietary dead-hand. The Quaker believed that a continuing revelation of Truth would be vouchsafed to those who performed their duty in obedience to the Light Within.

To appreciate what has been called the "theocratic democracy" in Pennsylvania as contrasted with the "theocratic oligarchy" of the Bay State, we may look at the famous Preface to the First Frame of Government adopted in England in 1682. In this Preface Penn bases government squarely upon God's law: "Such as would not live conformable to the holy law within, should fall under the reproof and correction, of the just law without, in a judicial administration." Then he quotes St. Paul that "the powers that be are ordained of God etc."

For Penn "this settles the divine right of government beyond exception, and that for two ends:
first, to terrify evil-doers; secondly, to cherish
those who do well; which gives government a
life beyond corruption, and makes it as durable
in the world as good men shall be." It is then
no surprise, but very significant, to find him
writing "Government seems to me a part of
religion itself, a thing sacred in its institution
and end." That statement at once stamps Penn's
intention to treat government as a religious
enterprise.

Morally, Penn was as much a Puritan as the
founders of the oldest New England colonies.
Like them, he based his policy on christianity
as a revealed religion. Penn's religion, however,
was not bound with bands of iron, but was
expansive and inclusive of other faiths. Thus,
the founding Fathers of the Republic with their
"natural religion" of the Age of Enlightenment
found nothing in Penn which they could not
adopt.

Unfortunately, that governments are not better
than they are is the fault of men who "side with
their passions against their reason, and their

sinister interests have so strong a bias upon
their minds, that they lean to them against the
good of the things they know."[81] Despite this
acquaintance with human frailty, Penn's idealism
did not fail him. He thought that some good men
could be found, and such men were all that was
required to make any government function well.
As to the Quakers, so to Penn "the common
ideas of government", whether monarchy, aristocracy or democracy were not of primary concern: "any government is free to the people
under it (whatever be the frame) where the
laws rule, and the people are a party to those laws,
and more than this is tyranny, oligarchy and
confusion."[82]

We shall agree with Penn that the character
of men is more important than multiplicity of
laws in the conduct of good government, for
"governments, like clocks, go from the motion
men give them, and as governments are made
and moved by men, so by men they are ruined
too. Wherefore governments rather depend upon
men, than men upon governments. Let men be
good, and the government cannot be bad; if it
be ill, they will cure it. But if men be bad, let

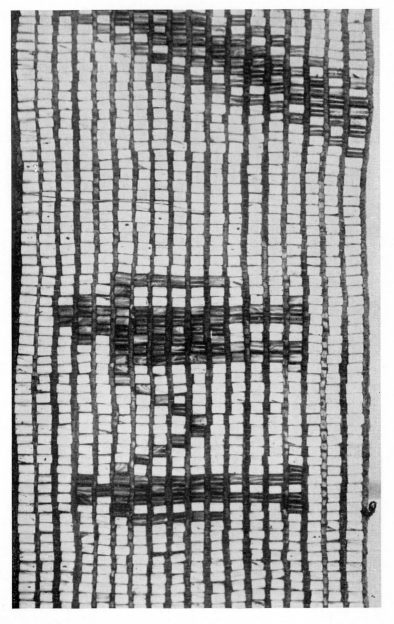

Center section of the Wampum Belt given to William Penn by the Indians.

the government be never so good, they will endeavour to warp and spoil it to their turn."[83]

The place to start, then, as we admit now, is with the individual citizen and "a virtuous education of youth", that there may be a succession of responsible citizens and of honorable magistrates in order that power may be supported in reverence with the people, and the people secured from the abuse of power, for "liberty without obedience is confusion, and obedience without liberty is slavery."[84] Believing in the necessity of public education to promote civic virtue, Penn did not delay to grant a charter pursuant to which there were presently incorporated fifteen "Overseers of the Public School founded by charter in the town and county of Philadelphia in Pennsylvania." The William Penn Charter School now in Germantown and Friends Select School now located on the Parkway are the two modern historical survivors of Penn's provision.

In the Preamble of the Great Law enacted at Chester, or Upland as it had been earlier called, upon Penn's arrival in 1682, it is again stated that "the glory of Almighty God and the good of mankind, is the reason and end of government, and therefore, government in itself is a venerable ordinance of God." In the first chapter of the Great Law, just as in the case of Rhode Island already quoted, complete religious liberty is guaranteed, with no obligation "to frequent or maintain any religious worship, place or ministry whatever contrary" to one's mind, but to have Christian liberty in that respect. There was, thus, to be no established church of any kind and no tithes. It is only God, the only Lord of conscience, Father of Lights and Spirits who "can enlighten the mind, and persuade and convince the understandings of people."

In the last and final Charter of Privileges granted by Penn in 1701, before his second departure from Philadelphia, the same guarantees are repeated, "because no people can be truly happy tho' under the greatest enjoyment of civil liberties, if abridged of the Freedom of their Consciences, as to their religious Profession and Worship." In this charter under which Pennsylvania lived longer than it has under any other, the Proprietor repeats as before that no one shall be molested or prejudiced for any conscientious

persuasion or practice, nor be compelled to do
or suffer any act or thing contrary to his religious persuasion. And it is further declared
that "all Persons who also profess to believe
in Jesus Christ, the Saviour of the world, shall
be capable . . . to serve this Government in any
Capacity, both legislatively and executively, he
or they solemnly promising, when lawfully
required, Allegiance to the King as Sovereign,
and Fidelity to the Proprietary and Governor,
and taking the Attests as now established by
the Law made at Newcastle" in 1700. It will
be observed that professed Christians only may
hold office, while all inhabitants who confess
and acknowledge God are free to live quietly
in accordance with their respective consciences
under the civil government. Also, a solemn
promise is an acceptable substitute for a qualify-
ing oath out of consideration for the Quaker
conscience in this respect.

There is a good deal of religious language in
the significant documents quoted, but it will be
observed that it is all used to prove that government is founded upon religion, and that the form
taken by religion in the individual case is to

be respected. A decade earlier in 1670 Penn had thus expressed the Quaker loyalty toward government and law except when the religious conscience was affected: "We acknowledge government to be necessary, because of transgressors. Secondly, that this government should consist of wholesome laws, to suppress vice and immoral practices, as oaths, whoredoms, murders, lies, thefts, extortion, treachery, profaneness, defamation, and the like ungodly and immodest actions; and in the encouragement of men contrarily qualified: these are fundamentals in law and gospel. In short, we heartily own the English Government upon its ancient civil basis. Thirdly, that there be many other temporary laws suited to State emergency in civil matters, as in trade, etc., to which we also account ourselves obliged. Fourthly, that we there only dissent, where conscience in point of faith and worship towards God is concerned."[85]

There is no need at this distance of time to record the provisions of Penn for the usual machinery of government and of justice. The reserved interests of the Proprietor were of course soon eliminated, and complete self-government by the people, as he intended, had taken effect. Justice was to be tempered with mercy as it now is, and honest government was to be provided by virtuous citizens trained to carry their responsibilities. We may, however, get a clearer idea of the conditions under which our predecessors lived in Pennsylvania, if we present in some detail specific examples of how Penn's Quaker principles were applied in his laws:

1. The Assembly was to meet on a certain date, with authority to adjourn at its own will, and with power to amend the constitution. [At this time Parliament met and was dismissed at the whim of the king.]

2. The avoidance of war was provided for through Assembly control of tax legislation. As long as Quakers predominated in the Assembly, no taxation for war purposes could be expected.

3. Capital punishment was restricted to punishment for treason and murder. [Sir James Fitzjames Stephen in his *History of the Criminal Law of England*[86] is authority for the statement that toward the end of the seventeenth century in England the following were capital crimes: high treason, petty treason, piracy, murder, arson,

burglary, house-breaking and putting in fear, highway robbery, horse stealing, stealing from the person above the value of a shilling, rape and abduction with intent to marry. In the case of persons who could not read, all felonies, including manslaughter, every kind of theft above the value of a shilling, and all robbery were capital crimes. Compared with such a bloodthirsty code, the humanitarian limitations of the Quaker Penn are evident.]

4. Freedom of worship and liberty of conscience were guaranteed.

5. An affirmation had the same legal value as an oath.

6. The accused was guaranteed a free and open trial by his peers, at a minimum of expense, with the same privilege of witnesses and counsel as his prosecutors.

7. All persons wrongfully imprisoned or prosecuted at law should have double damages against the informer or prosecutor.

8. The abolishment of imprisonment for debt and of jailer's fees was provided for.

9. The opportunity to work in private cells replaced idleness in common jails.

10. Quaker marriages were declared to be legal.

11. The Indians were to be treated humanely and justly as men and brothers.

12. The education of children over twelve years of age was provided for "to the end that none may be idle, but the poor may work to live, and the rich, if they become poor, may not want."

13. A public employment agency was to be set up.

14. Scandal-mongers were to be punished.

15. Gaming, bear-baiting, cock-fighting, etc., were forbidden.

16. Representative government was guaranteed by voters over twenty-one years of age possessed of a minimum property.

Aside from regulations covering the government itself, there we have the provisions of Pennsylvania law which directly affected the life of its citizens. Not of peculiar concern to them were Penn's later published plans for the substitution of international arbitration for war which he proposed in his *Essay towards the Present and Future Peace of Europe* (1693), and his statesmanlike *Plan for the Union of the Colonies*

(1697). Both of these projects are of historical importance: inspired by religious and humanitarian motives, the first is the most impressive proposal for international cooperation made by anyone before the League of Nations; of the second it has recently been said that all the matters placed by this plan at the disposition of a central body found their place in the Articles of Confederation a century later.[87] There are seven articles in Penn's plan of 1697, while there are thirteen Articles of Confederation of 1777. After proposing that each of the ten colonies appoint two persons "well qualified for sense, sobriety and substance" to act as its representatives in a Congress presided over by the King's Commissioner to meet once a year or more often, Penn proceeds to the following important paragraph 6 describing the duties of such a Congress:

"That their business shall be to hear and adjust all matters of complaint or difference between province and province. As first, where persons quit their own province and go to another, that they may avoid their just debts tho they be able to pay them; second, where offenders fly justice, or justice cannot well be had upon such offenders in the provinces that entertain them; third, to prevent or cure injuries in point of commerce; fourth, to consider of ways and means to support the union and safety of these provinces against the public enemies. In which Congress the quotas of men and charges will be much easier, and more equally set, than it is possible for any establishment made here to do; for the provinces, knowing their own condition and one another's, can debate that matter with more freedom and satisfaction and better adjust and balance their affairs in all respects for their common safety."

These are the points later embodied in the Articles of Confederation, especially in Articles 4 and 8. There is no other founder of an American colony who has thus so early and so directly stated important functions of our federal government. As Thomas Jefferson said, Penn was "the first, either in ancient or modern times, who has laid the foundation of government in the pure and unadulterated principles of peace, of reason and right."[88]

No better proof of Penn's generous intentions for the liberties of his colonists could have been given than his provision for them of *The Excellent Priviledge of Liberty and Property*, thought to have been printed by Bradford at Philadelphia in 1687. In 1897 the Philobiblon Club of Philadelphia reprinted this *Priviledge* from the unique known copy now in the Haverford College Library. It is a remarkable gift for a Proprietor to make to his citizens. He "put the power in the people." His purpose is thus expressed in his address to the Reader: "the chief end of the publication hereof is for the information and understanding (what is their native right and inheritance) of such who may not have leisure from their Plantations to read large volumes." This text of Magna Charta with Penn's comments thereon is in fact a diminutive law library for the guidance of freemen and their legislators. As law books are hard to come by, Penn sends this "root from whence all our wholesome English Laws spring" in the hope that it may be of use to the settlers and determine them "not to give away anything of Liberty and Property that at present they do, (or of right as loyal English Subjects, ought to) enjoy, but take up the good example of our ancestors, and understand, that it is easy to part with or give away great privileges, but hard to be gained, if once lost."

In his *Introduction* Penn goes on to say: "This original happy Frame of Government is truly and properly called *an Englishman's Liberty*" and is his birthright, as shines most conspicuously in two things: Parliaments and Juries. In Parliament the subject has a share through his chosen Representatives in the Legislative Power; through Juries he has a share in the executive part of the law. "These two grand pillars of English liberty are the Fundamental Vital Privileges, whereby we have been, and are preserved more free and happy than any other people in the world, and (we trust) shall ever continue so."

Penn's persistent insistence upon the authority of Magna Charta is explained by the fact that he found there the best argument for that freedom of conscience and worship which he sought for himself and his Friends. As the editor of the Philobiblon Club edition, the late Frederick D. Stone, well says: "In defending the right of his followers to worship God according to the dictates of their conscience, he based his argu-

ments on Magna Charta, feeling that this was
the only foundation upon which the religious
liberty he contended for could safely rest, and
that if he could gain for the Quakers a full
recognition of their rights as free Englishmen,
that liberty would be secure."

Less well known than the preceding documents is this final evidence of Penn's prophetic
proposed settlement of national claims. In 1709
he addressed a letter to the Duke of Marlborough
then leading Britain's armies in the war with the
French. The letter touches upon the territories
claimed by England and France on the American
continent, and proposes a natural boundary
which after the vicissitudes of war has prevailed
between Canada and the United States. He
wrote to the Duke: "I send this in reference to
our northern bounds in America. The English
Empire on the continent lies upon the south
side, and we claim to the North Sea of Hudson's
Bay; but I should be glad if our north bounds
might be expressed and allowed to the south side
of St. Lawrence's River that feeds Canada
eastward, and comes from the lakes westward;
which will make a glorious country, and from

those lakes due west to the River Mississippi, and travers that river to the extreme bounds of the continent westward; whereby we may secure one thousand miles of that river down to the Bay of Mexico, and that the French demolish, or, at least, quit all their settlements within the bounds aforesaid.

"Without such a settlement of our American bounds, we shall be in hazard of being dangerously surprised at one time or other, by the French and their Indians."[89]

Here was a practical application of a "live and let live" policy which Penn had laid down for arbitration in 1693: "Something everybody must be willing to give or quit, that he may keep the rest, and by this establishment be forever freed from the necessity of losing more."[90]

It was said earlier that it is difficult in short compass to cover all the activities of William Penn and to do justice to the many sides of his personality. For example, one could speak at greater length of his intellectual equipment. His surviving letter to Sir John Rodes, a young Quaker gentleman of Yorkshire, in 1693 reveals a very wide acquaintance, not with the drama and poetry which as a Quaker of the time he would have disparaged, but with the classics and standard works in many fields of learning.[91]

Beside his academic culture, he was greatly interested in the cultivation of flowers, fruits and vines and in landscaping. Not only do his letters about the natural riches of Pennsylvania and his directions for the planting of Pennsbury give evidence of this; before his first visit to his province he was already elected one of the earliest members of the Royal Society.

He also had claims as a pioneer in city planning, and Philadelphia after two centuries and a half has developed along the lines laid down by his commissioners and his surveyor Thomas Holme. He appreciated also the importance of leaving wood-lots in the midst of cleared land.

As an author he is by no means negligible. His *No Cross, No Crown*, a Quaker classic for two centuries, can still make the complacent Christian wince at the inconsistencies of his life. But his most notable contribution to literature is his *Fruits of Solitude* and the recently collected *Fruits of an Active Life*, consisting in all of over one thousand epigrammatic reflections upon religion, morals, government, education, toleration and related topics. These are the reactions of a profoundly religious man caught up in human society.

Penn's attitude toward the Indians has been so frequently praised as to make little reference to it necessary at this late date. This attitude of brotherly good will has been shown to be but one manifestation of Quaker philosophy. As the late Professor Hull pointed out in his topical biography of the Founder, Penn's early project for the trial of Indians by a mixed jury of whites and natives, his provision for three arbitrators at each county court, his proposal in 1693 for a European congress of nations which should settle disputes through arbitration, and his plan for the union of the colonies in 1697,—"are interesting stepping-stones towards the peaceful international settlement of international disputes."

An effort has been made to sum up the rights of humanity in a diminishing world by the statement called "The Atlantic Charter". No document could have more deeply interested William Penn or more surely engaged his cooperation.

His philosophy would have been challenged by each of the four freedoms as conceived by representatives of the countries which have most closely followed his advanced humanitarian principles. The right to freedom of speech and freedom of worship has been fairly well recognized in civilized countries. Freedom from want has not been achieved because of human selfishness and man's economic ineptitude. Freedom from fear is as yet unattained and will remain so, Penn would point out, so long as we place physical power above spiritual forces in the relations of man with man.

Penn would insist that we are proceeding according to a false philosophy, and that peaceful relations are produced by evidences of good will, not by swinging a big stick or threatening with atomic bombs. The peoples want peace, but to secure it their leaders are afraid to trust the Christian principles they profess. Penn's Christian philosophy is set forth in the closing *Fruits of Solitude*, and as applied to relations among men is summed up in the plea: "Let us then try what Love will do: for if men did once see we love them, we should soon find they

Charter of Pennsylvania

WILLIAM PENN

J.J. Barralet Direxit.   Lawson sculp.

Drawn from the Original Bust in the Loganian Library Philadelphia 1 Nov.r 1797

would not harm us."[92] This of course is a truth which is not yet trusted by the leaders of even Christian nations. But it is the only step toward civil and national peace which has not yet been given a thorough trial. It is just possible, as Penn thought, that the principle may work among men of good will. Penn's principles have been admired and adopted in so many other respects that it is possible he was right also in his approach to freedom from fear.

So long ago as 1844 in a Fourth of July oration in the very city where four Quakers had been hanged in the seventeenth century, Charles Sumner reminded his fellow-citizens of Boston: "To William Penn belongs the distinction, destined to brighten as men advance in virtue, of first in human history establishing the *Law of Love* as a rule of conduct in intercourse of nations."

REFERENCE NOTES.

[1] American Heroes and Hero-Worship. Harper & Bros., N. Y. and London, 1943, pp. 25-26.

[2] Poulson's American Daily Advertiser for October 28, 1826.

[3] Cf. J. B. Stoudt, The Liberty Bells of Pennsylvania, Phila., 1930, pp. 37-58.

[4] R. M. Jones, Spiritual Reformers of the XVI and XVII Centuries.

[5] An Address to Protestants, 1679.

[6] Journal (Bicentenary ed.), London, 1891, I, 11.

[7] A Key Opening the Way, 1692.

[8] A Serious Apology, 1671.

[9] A Letter to the Council and Senate of the City of Emden, 1674.

[10] The Great Case of Liberty of Conscience, 1670.

[11] Ibid.

[12] Memoirs of John Whiting (1655-1722) 2nd ed., pp. 68-69.

[13] Works, I, 6.

[14] The New Athenians No Noble Bereans, 1692.

[15] Some Fruits of Solitude, No. 498.

[16] The Spirit of Truth Vindicated, 1672.

[17] Epistle 17, 1652.

[18] Journal (Bicentenary Ed.), London, 1891, II, 340-341.

[19] To the Children of Light, 1678.

[20] Quakerism a New Nickname, 1672.

[21] Ibid.

[22] A Serious Apology, 1671.

[23] The Christian Quaker, 1673.

[24] Reason Against Railing, 1673.

[25] An Address to Protestants, 1679.

[26] Quakerism a New Nickname, 1672.

[27] Wisdom Justified of her Children, 1673.

[28] No Cross, No Crown, 1669.

[29] Journal, (Bicentenary ed.) I, 99.

[30] Lectures on Modern History, London, 1906, p. 223.

[31] Thomas Clarkson, Memoirs of the Private and Public Life of William Penn, London, 1813, II, 38-39.

32 Works, I, 154.

33 Diary for August 30, 1664.

34 Ibid. for August 26, 1664.

35 Travails in Holland and Germany, 1694.

36 S. M. Janney, Life of William Penn, 1st ed., Phila., 1852, p. 163.

37 The Friend (Phila.) VI (1833), 257-8.

38 Janney, Penn, p. 163.

39 The Great Case of Liberty of Conscience, 1670.

40 A Letter to the Council and Senate of the City of Emden, 1674.

41 Ibid.

42 R. M. Jones, The Quakers in the American Colonies, N. Y., 1911, p. XIII Note.

43 Mem. Hist. Soc. Pa., vol. I, pt. I, p. 203.

44 Samuel Smith, History of New Jersey, 80-81.

45 History of the U. S., pt. II, ch. XVI.

46 Janney, Penn, 82.

47 Janney, Penn, 556.

48 Mem. Hist. Soc. Pa., IX, 280.

49 Mem. Hist. Soc. Pa., X, 71.

50 Id., IX, 102.

51 Travails in Holland and Germany, 1694.

52 Penn, Works, I, 6.

53 Ibid. I, 39.

54 Letter to Justices in Middlesex, 1674.

55 Janney, Penn, 170.

56 Ibid., 163.

57 Ibid., 166.

58 Ibid., 213.

59 Mem. Hist. Soc. Pa., II, I, 245.

60 Mem. Hist. Soc. Pa., I, II, 421.

61 Janney, Penn, 249.

62 Clarkson, Penn, I, 418.

63 Mem. Hist. Soc. Pa., IX, 79.

64 Hist. of the United States, pt. II, ch. XVI.

[65] All quotations of charters and laws of this chapter are from Thorpe, The Federal and State Constitutions.

[66] Mere Literature and Other Essays, 1897, p. 218.

[67] Mem. Hist. Soc. Pa., I, I, 201-2.

[68] Mem. Hist. Soc. Pa., I, I, 202-204.

[69] England's Great Interest in the Choice of a New Parliament, 1679.

[70] Ibid.

[71] England's Present Interest Discovered, 1675.

[72] An Address to Protestants, 1679.

[73] Speech to the Council, 1700.

[74] Mem. Hist. Soc. Pa., III, II, 205.

[75] Janney, Penn, 166.

[76] Fox, Epistle 106.

[77] Fox, Epistle 162.

[78] Spirit of Laws, BK. IV, Ch. VII.

[79] Mem. Hist. Soc. Pa., IX, 373.

[80] Mem. Hist. Soc. Pa., IX, 374.

[81] Preface of First Frame of Government of Pennsylvania, 1682.

[82] Ibid.

[83] Ibid.

[84] Ibid.

[85] Truth Rescued from Imposture, 1670.

[86] I, 467.

[87] Cf. Merrill Jensen, The Articles of Confederation, 107.

[88] Poulson's American Daily Advertiser for October 28, 1826.

[89] Mem. Hist. Soc. Pa., III, I, 291-292.

[90] Essay Towards the Present and Future Peace of Europe, 1693.

[91] Mrs. Godfrey Locker-Lampson, A Quaker Post-Bag, London, 1910.

[92] No. 545.

NOTES ON THE ILLUSTRATIONS

The three engraved maps and the lithographic portrait and the four engraved portraits are reproduced from originals in the collection of the Penn Mutual.

The end papers at the front of the book reproduce a section of a Sanson map of North America, dated 1669, showing how "America" would look to William Penn at about the time he first considered the possibility of colonizing there. From the cartouche on the map:—

AMERIQUE
SEPTENTRIONALE

Par N. Sanson Geographe Ord.^{re} du Roy.
Revenue et changee en plusieurs endroits
suivant les Memoires les plus recents.
Par G. Sanson Geogr. Ordinaire du Roy.
a Paris
Chez Pierre Mariette rue St. Iacques a l'Efperace
Avec privilege de fa Mai.^{re} pour20-Ans.
1669.

The end papers at the back of the book reproduce a detail of a Homanno map of the Mississippi region of North America, dated 1687. Showing the British Colonies, this is an early appearance of Pennsylvania within six years after William Penn had founded his province.
From the cartouche on the map :—

Ampliflimæ Regionis
MISSISSIPPI
Seu
PROVINCIÆ LUDOVICIANÆ
a R. P. Ludovico Hennepin Francisc. Miff.
In America Septentrionali
Anno 1687 Detectæ.
nunc Gallorum Coloniis et Actionum Ne-
gotiis toto Orbe celeberrimæ,
Nova Tabula
edita
a IO. BAPT. HOMANNO S.C.M. Geographo
Norimbergæ.
Cum Privilegio Sac. Cæf. Maj.

Opposite page 2.

A texture photograph by Philip B. Wallace of Philadelphia showing a detail of the bronze Liberty Bell. The original crack in the Bell was drilled out to prevent spreading, but the crack nevertheless continued, as is clearly shown.

Opposite page 10.

A photograph by Photo Illustrators, Philadelphia, (copyright) showing a night view of the statue of William Penn atop City Hall, Philadelphia, with the silhouette of the statue thrown by searchlights against a bank of clouds.

Opposite page 50.

Lithograph by Charles R. Gardner after the portrait of "Penn in Armor," painted by an unknown artist, showing William Penn in 1666. The painting is in the collection of the Historical Society of Pennsylvania.

Opposite page 58.

Engraving of Admiral Sir William Penn, father of William Penn the founder. Engraved by C. Turner after the portrait by Sir P. Lely. "Admiral Penn, One of Cromwell's Admirals who took Jamaica from the Spaniards, from the Original Picture, London, Published by S. Woodburn, 1811."

Opposite page 74.

Engraving by Petr. Dreret of the Vander Werff portrait of King Charles II.

Opposite page 90.

Engraving by R. Sheppard of the G. Kneller portrait of King James II.

Opposite page 106.

Reproduced also is a Holme survey may of "Pensilvania in America," the so-called Willdey Map, London, of 1717. Philadelphia County, Bucks County, Chester County are shown, and set in is the plan for the City of Philadelphia. "The Proprietaryes Mannor of Penns-berry" is near the lower right hand corner of the map.

Opposite page 122.

A texture photograph by Philip B. Wallace of the center design of the famous wampum belt given by the Indians to William Penn, and now in the collection of the Historical Society of Pennsylvania.

Opposite page 138.

Engraving by Lawson of the J. J. Barralet picture after the Bevan portrait of William Penn drawn from the original bust in the Loganian Library, Philadelphia, 1797.

Benjamin Franklin, while in London in 1760, searching for a portrait of William Penn, wrote:—"Sylvanus Bevan, an Old Quaker apothecary, remarkable for the notice he takes of countenances, and a knack of cutting in ivory strong likenesses of persons he has once seen, hearing of Lord Cobham's desire, set himself to recollect Penn's face, with which he had been well acquainted; and cut a little bust of him in ivory, which he sent to Lord Cobham, without any letter or notice that it was Penn's. But my Lord, who had personally known Penn, on seeing it, immediately cried out, 'Whence comes this? It is William Penn himself!'"

Penn died almost half a century before silhouettes became the mode, therefore we inherited no shadow portrait of him. But today, two centuries later, the outline can be traced from the profile in ivory by Bevan, and a conventionalized silhouette made as you see it in the frontispiece of this book.